STRAND PRICE
$ 5.00

D1068351

"Because we were ready and willing, we were able to bring about one of the largest mass migrations in Jewish history."

— **PETER W. MAY**
CHAIRMAN, OPERATION EXODUS
UJA-FEDERATION OF NEW YORK

"The response of the New York Jewish community was phenomenal. It is because of that support that we were able to provide freedom to so many of our people."

— **ALEXANDER E. FISHER**
CO-CHAIRMAN, OPERATION EXODUS
UJA-FEDERATION OF NEW YORK

# OPERATION EXODUS

## THE MAKING OF A MIRACLE

FOREWORD BY
**PETER W. MAY**

TEXT BY
**DENA MERRIAM**

PHOTOGRAPHS BY
**ZION OZERI**

PUBLISHED BY
**UJA-FEDERATION OF NEW YORK**

BUT THEY'RE NOT HOME FREE YET.

Center

OPERATION EXODUS

UJA-FEDERATION

# DEDICATION

This book is dedicated to all of those whose support of UJA-Federation of New York has made *Operation Exodus* possible, and to those whose continued support of UJA-Federation's Annual Campaign will enable our work of rescue and resettlement of Jews to go on. The enormous success of this operation can be attributed to: the hard work, generosity and enthusiasm of so many individuals and families within the UJA-Federation network, as well as from religious schools, day schools, country clubs, the various religious streams, companies in various UJA-Federation divisions who sponsored Freedom Flights or conducted other special projects; the UJA-Federation Russian Division and all other divisions within the UJA-Federation family working directly with Jews from the former Soviet Union; UJA-Federation professional and support staff; and all 130 UJA-Federation overseas and domestic beneficiary agencies. The crisis continues for Jews living in Russia and the surrounding republics. It is essential for us to keep up the momentum, helping Jews, one by one, escape to a better life in Israel. Because of your support through UJA-Federation's Annual Campaign, we will be able to respond to the needs of these Jews, as well as to the needs of Jews around the world .

Operation Exodus: The Making of a Miracle



Designed and Produced by Ruder•Finn Inc.

UJA-Federation Coordinators: Gail J. Hyman, Executive Director, Marketing & Communications
Lynne Calman, Director of Special Projects

*UJA-Federation of New York gratefully acknowledges the many individuals and organizations whose cooperation and counsel helped to shape this book.*

Frontispiece: New Yorkers on a UJA-Federation mega-mission to Israel welcome Jews from the former Soviet Union as they step onto the tarmac at Ben Gurion Airport; Previous spread: UJA-Federation of New York supporters march at a Salute to Israel Solidarity Parade holding large *tzedakah* boxes, which were used to raise money for *Operation Exodus, photograph by Alan Rosenberg;* Page 10*:* A group of New Yorkers from the *Coalition to Free Soviet Jews,* a UJA-Federation-supported organization, march in the 1987 Freedom Sunday Rally for Soviet Jews in Washington, D.C.

All photographs in this book were printed by David Wong Custom Photo Lab of New York City.

Production assistance by Studio Gribaudo
Printed in Italy by Poligrafiche Bolis s.p.a. - Bergamo

# CONTENTS

# FOREWORD

This book, which so movingly recounts the history of UJA-Federation's *Operation Exodus* Campaign, is a testimony to the importance and enormous success of this undertaking. It is a confirmation of the critical role we, the New York Jewish community, played in bringing it about. The photographs displayed in the following pages will help us to remember what it was that inspired us to pull together as a community and raise the large sums of money needed for this rescue and resettlement operation. Through our efforts, we were able to guarantee freedom to hundreds of thousands of our people.

It may take years to fully realize the historic import of *Operation Exodus* which, within the span of just a few years, rescued hundreds of thousands of Jews and brought a dramatic increase in population to Israel, infusing the country with new talent and resources. For those who grew up in the shadow of the Holocaust, the ability to band together and bring about this momentous event is a great achievement. It proves the strength and commitment of the Jewish community.

As Chairman of the UJA-Federation *Operation Exodus* campaign, I am deeply grateful for the tremendous support, enthusiasm and generosity of the New York Jewish community. Without your extensive involvement in this campaign, it would not have been a success. This took hard work and persistence, but we can take pride in the fact that we were able to turn what was a dangerous situation for so many Jews into the positive outcome of freedom in Israel.

The story of the exodus of Jews from the former Soviet Union is not over. Hundreds of thousands of Jews remain in Russia and the surrounding republics, and many of these people, fearful of the still uncertain environment in that part of the world, are hoping to make *aliyah*. UJA-Federation depends on the continued support of all of us to meet the rescue and resettlement needs of this population.

There are not many opportunities in a lifetime where one can participate in changing the course of world events. The rescue of our people from the former Soviet Union and Ethiopia presented such an opportunity. Through our united efforts, we were able to create one of the largest mass migrations in the history of our people — an event that will create a sense of pride and achievement for generations of Jews to come.

It is tremendously gratifying to know that, because of our work, many hundreds of thousands of our people are now able to create not only a brighter future for themselves and their families but, also, a stronger and more secure future for all of world Jewry through the commitment and resources they bring to Israel.

**PETER W. MAY**
CHAIRMAN, OPERATION EXODUS
UJA-FEDERATION OF NEW YORK

COALITION TO FREE SOVIET JEWS
The City that
Never Sleeps
Never Stops Fighting
for Soviet Jews

# OPERATION EXODUS:
## THE MAKING OF A MIRACLE

The 4,000-year history of the Jews is a story of continuous migrations. Since forced from our homeland nearly 2,000 years ago, Jews have founded communities on all continents, and when the modern state of Israel was formed in 1948, the migrations were reversed. The history of that young nation has been one of steady ingathering, where Jews returned to live again in an ancient homeland. One of the most dramatic chapters in this recent history is the migration of over 700,000* Jews from the former Soviet Union to Israel. This represents the largest movement of Jews in a generation, possibly since the founding of Israel, and the count is not over. Jews from the former Soviet Union continue to arrive in Israel at the rate of 5,000 or 6,000 a month, and the predictions are that the total number will soon surpass one million.

During this same period, another small piece in the mosaic of Jewish history has also been redeemed. Twenty-nine thousand Jews from Ethiopia, cut off from their homeland for 2,500 years, have been rescued from their remote communities and resettled in Israel. Combined, these two phenomena have tremendous implications for Israel, foreshadowing a brighter and more secure future for world Jewry. While the long-term impact on Israel can only be surmised, the short-term needs present an immediate and urgent reality. The benefit of this surge of new arrivals depends in no small part on Israel's ability to absorb this sizable population.

This recent migration to Israel represents a major event in the annals of Jewish communal life. Perhaps for the first time, Jews from around the world have been able to participate in changing world events to our advantage as Jews. Clearly, the lessons of the Holocaust have been learned.

*Operation Exodus*, the worldwide fund-raising campaign that helped make possible this unprecedented migration, has proven that Jews will not sit idly by while other Jews are threatened. Working in conjunction with the national office of the United Jewish Appeal (UJA), local Federations aroused the support of Jewish communities throughout the country.

The financial and emotional support provided by Jews in the United States through *Operation Exodus* has enabled hundreds of thousands of Jews to escape from oppression and begin a new life in Israel. Within

* The number at the time of publication. The approximate number of Jews from the former Soviet Union who made *aliyah* to Israel during the four-year duration of *Operation Exodus* is 500,000. All statistics quoted in this book are approximate figures based on data released at the time of publication.

the space of only a few years, American Jewry raised nearly one billion dollars for this historic rescue and resettlement operation. The leadership role of UJA-Federation of New York was and continues to be critical, not only in terms of the 177.5 million dollars it raised but, also, in providing desperately needed services, and doing so with great enthusiasm and a deep sense of commitment. Because of the large Jewish population in the New York vicinity, UJA-Federation of New York was able to raise more money than any other local Federation. Much of this money went to two of its major overseas beneficiaries — the Jewish Agency For Israel (JAFI) and the American Jewish Joint Distribution Committee (JDC), both of which assumed direct responsibility for resettling refugees from the former Soviet Union.

The partnership created through *Operation Exodus* between Jews from the former Soviet Union, Israel and the United States has created a model of Jewish unity that hopefully will remain alive for many years to come.

## THE OPPRESSION OF JEWS: LIFE IN THE FORMER SOVIET UNION

For as long as Jews have lived in the Soviet Union, they have met with anti-Semitism and persecution. A history of periodic pogroms dating back centuries has haunted Jews in that part of the world. During World War II, the Nazis lined up and killed hundreds of thousands of Jews in the Ukraine with the tacit support of many Ukrainians. After the death of Stalin in 1953, anti-Semitism assumed a more subtle form but remained a force in Soviet society nonetheless: Jews were not admitted to certain universities; many could not advance in their careers; Jewish children were made to feel like outsiders in their neighborhoods and schools; families had to keep secret their Jewish heritage; Jewish cemeteries were desecrated; and Jews were required to list Hebrew as their nationality on their identification cards. Also, it was illegal to teach Hebrew, get married under a *chupah*, and celebrate the Jewish holidays. These pernicious but less overt forms of anti-Semitism were pervasive and ongoing.

After Israel's victory in the Six-Day War of 1967, Jews around the world experienced renewed pride in being Jewish. In the United States, Jews became increasingly concerned about the violation of the rights of our people. The former Soviet Union, home to the third largest population of Jews in the world, was an area of special concern. In 1974, the United States government took its first stand on the issue of Soviet Jewry, passing the Jackson-Vanik Amendment, which linked trade with the emigration of Jews from the former Soviet Union: the Soviets would receive favorable trade status if they permitted Jews and other persecuted minorities to leave the country. The Amendment became law in 1975. Also during this time period, the Helsinki Final Act was signed. The United States and the Soviet Union were among the signatories: this agreement described what the West considered to be a proper regard for human rights, including the freedoms of speech and press and the right to emigrate, especially for Soviet Jews. As a result of these two major initiatives, Moscow committed itself to liberalizing travel and emigration policies for its citizens. Jews began to leave the former Soviet Union in growing numbers during the latter part of the 1970s, a decade that also witnessed increased public awareness of the plight of the "refuseniks."

Refuseniks were Jews who were trying to leave the former Soviet Union but whose right of emigration was denied by the government. They embarked on a mission to publicize their situation, and gained significant support in the West. The reaction of the Soviet government to this public outcry was harassment and, in some cases, arrest.

Natan Sharansky, perhaps the most prominent of this group, became a symbol of the plight of Soviet Jewry. Sentenced to 13 years in prison in 1978 on the charge of "treason," Sharansky succeeded in attracting the attention and support of Jews and intellectuals the world over. His wife, Avital, was often a speaker at rallies for Soviet Jewry, helping to arouse enormous public response and support for the cause. Unable to ignore rising pressure from the United States, the Soviet government permitted over 200,000 Jews to emigrate between 1971 and 1979.

Following the Soviet invasion of Afghanistan in 1979, the policy of détente between the United States and the former Soviet Union came to a halt, and the emigration of Jews slowed to a trickle. The Soviets officially established an Anti-Zionist Committee aimed at increasing their propaganda against what they called the "criminal activity of international Zionism," further endangering the safety of Jews living in that country. The responsibility for the well-being of those Jews now fell onto the shoulders of Israel, the Jewish community in the United States, and the rest of the Jewish world. UJA-Federation began to accelerate its efforts to publicize the oppression of Jews in the former Soviet Union, and it assumed the role of providing for the basic needs of Jews living there.

During the middle years of the 1980s, the former Soviet Union began to undergo the birth pangs of change. In the face of their crumbling economic and political situation, they made an effort to rid the country of dissidents, alternating periods of slackened and tightened emigration practices.

In the late 1980s, with the policies of Perestroika and Glasnost (internal political and economic programs of reform), U.S.-Soviet relations improved as the Soviets attempted to establish a more open society. Increased freedom of speech brought many benefits to the population, but it also brought a more vocal and popular anti-Semitism.

Anti-Semitism no longer was government policy; it became the practice of the streets. Anti-Semitic posters began appearing on walls in cities throughout the country, and groups of people shouting anti-Semitic slogans became more common. The specter of fear began to rise again for Jews. Never fully accepted by Soviet society, Jews now began to worry that the future might bring something even worse than they had known in the past. The emergence of Pamyat, the most active anti-Semitic group, was frighteningly reminiscent of Nazi gangs in Germany during the 1930s.

The environment became so unsettling that when Gorbachev once again opened the doors to emigration in 1989-90, Jews responded with a fervor, willing to accept great sacrifices in exchange for their freedom. Allowed to leave with no more than 140 dollars and two suitcases, Jews flocked in droves to the train stations and airports of Moscow.

## THE CALL TO ACTION: NEW YORK RESPONDS

By the end of 1989, it became clear that the departure of such large numbers of Jews from the former Soviet Union had created a crisis. Tremendous sums of money were needed to help with the rescue and resettlement effort. Based on the actions of the former Soviet government, there was no way of knowing how long the doors of emigration would remain open. There was a widespread feeling that anyone who wanted to leave should do so immediately.

During the 1970s, UJA-Federation had already begun to help the New York Jewish community mobilize itself by funding two organizations formed to publicize the plight of Soviet Jews: The Greater New York

Conference on Soviet Jewry, later renamed the Greater New York Coalition for Soviet Jewry, and the National Conference on Soviet Jewry. (The Student Struggle for Soviet Jewry was also formed during this period.) Nearly nine million dollars were allocated to these two organizations between 1970 and 1995.

To heighten public awareness of the problem, these groups used some of the same tactics employed by the civil rights movement of the 1960s. They organized rallies, distributed badges and arm bracelets calling for the freedom of Soviet Jews, and smuggled out letters from refuseniks depicting the pervasiveness of anti-Semitism in the former Soviet Union. Solidarity Sunday, held in New York City and also funded by UJA-Federation, was evidence of the growing unity among Jews behind this cause.

A landmark event was the Freedom Sunday Rally for Soviet Jews on December 6, 1987, when over 250,000 gathered in Washington, D.C. to meet Mikhail Gorbachev. In response, Gorbachev released several longtime refuseniks, including Ida Nudel and Vladimir Slepak. The activities of American Jewry were clearly having an effect, but it was still not enough. The call to release the refuseniks now changed into a forceful demand to free all Jews living in the former Soviet Union. When Gorbachev finally responded by opening the doors to emigration in 1989, UJA had to find a way to meet the sharply increased need for money and resettlement services.

Early in 1989, national UJA initiated its *Passage to Freedom* effort in New York and around the country. The campaign raised 46 million dollars by the end of that year, which was far short of what was needed to finance the tremendous exodus that had begun to get underway. The crisis was becoming increasingly severe. Large numbers of Jews were rushing at the opportunity to make *aliyah*. National UJA decided to launch a massive fund-raising campaign to help make possible this rescue and resettlement operation.

New York's Regency Hotel was the site for the national UJA kick-off breakfast in January of 1990, for what was to become the largest emergency fund-raising event in Jewish history. This breakfast, which was attended by a select number of major donors from around the country, initiated a monumental campaign to finance this historic exodus. During the first hour of the breakfast, donors pledged 53 million dollars.

Peter W. May was selected as campaign chairman for New York, Alexander E. Fisher as co-chairman. National UJA asked New York to set a goal of raising 75 million dollars. At the meeting of UJA-Federation of New York's Board of Directors on March 15, 1990, UJA-Federation leaders made an impassioned plea to support the urgent needs of Jews in the former Soviet Union. The response was overwhelming and, as a result, the New York goal was raised to 100 million dollars. Based on the large number of Jews who rallied to participate, it soon became apparent that even that goal would be surpassed. In March of that year, *Operation Exodus* was officially born.

As Jews from the former Soviet Union began to arrive in Israel and the U.S., they described the harassment they had experienced, the difficulties they had encountered in getting permission to leave, and the challenges they were facing in their new home. Their stories inundated the media, creating an emotionally charged atmosphere for the campaign. The New York Jewish community rallied to the aid of these new immigrants and, under the aegis of UJA-Federation of New York, many lay people developed innovative fund-raising programs that generated significant monies for the cause. As financial contributions mounted, there was unprecedented emotional support from the entire UJA-Federation of New York family for the Jews from the former Soviet Union.

## FREEDOM FLIGHTS: CARRYING JEWS TO ISRAEL

For many Jews living in the United States, one of the most dramatic moments of the whole *Operation Exodus* effort was the sight of Jews from the former Soviet Union descending the stairway of the Freedom Flight they had sponsored. This scene, repeated again and again, helped transform the Operation into a highly personal experience. It took on special meaning for every Jew who witnessed the event.

One of the early Freedom Flights was organized by a New York businessman, Mark Tsesarsky, a Jewish émigré who had left Kiev when he was 17 years old. Tsesarsky had risen to become a successful trader at Salomon Brothers Inc. and, in partnership with some 200 people from two major Wall Street firms, he organized a campaign to raise enough money for one of UJA-Federation of New York's first Freedom Flights. The budget of 250,000 dollars covered the cost of flying one jet filled with 250 Soviet Jews to Israel. The project was so successful that other corporations followed suit. New York donors were able to fly to Israel to greet their Freedom Flight and see first-hand the people whose passage they had sponsored, creating a bond between Jews en route to freedom and those who were making their *aliyah* possible.

Jews living in the United States were so moved by the stories coming out of the former Soviet Union that many wanted to see first-hand what Jews there were enduring. A number of lay leaders flew on missions to the former Soviet Union to witness what families were going through as they prepared to leave. During their stay in Uzbekistan or Ukraine, they helped families get their papers and possessions in order and flew with them to Israel, where they were able to share in their joy as they landed on Israeli soil. Groups of eager Israelis welcomed them as they descended their airplanes at Ben Gurion Airport.

To garner the support of Jews from the former Soviet Union whose freedom had already been secured, and who were established in the New York area, UJA-Federation established a Russian Division, with Lilly and Larry Wajnberg as the founding chairpeople. The Brighton Beach community in Brooklyn, a hub of Russian Jewish life and known as "little Odessa by the sea," became a center for fund-raising activities, contributing over 800,000 dollars to the New York campaign. The Russian Division sponsored an annual fund-raising dinner at the Manhattan Beach Jewish Center in Brooklyn, featuring many prominent Jews from the former Soviet Union, and calling media attention to the many Jewish immigrants who had developed successful businesses and were now able to give something back to the community. A grassroots effort of a fledgling immigrant community, their contributions were a testament to the gratitude they felt toward those who had made their freedom possible.

To maintain a high level of enthusiasm for, and involvement in, *Operation Exodus*, UJA-Federation of New York initiated a number of fund-raising concerts. One was "The Next Generation Concert," held at the Brooklyn Academy of Music in 1992. Produced by UJA-Federation, in conjunction with BAM and the Consulate General of Israel in New York, the festival premiered emerging Israeli performers, including émigrés from the former Soviet Union and Ethiopia.

The goal of *Operation Exodus* was to touch the hearts and souls of the entire Jewish community in the greater New York City area, and every level of contributor was able to participate. The *Operation Exodus* Certificate Program, conceived and initially funded by Irving and Nancy Silverman, enabled people to send in donations and receive certificates in honor of a person or occasion, or in memory of a loved one. National UJA developed other types of certificates with the inscription of one's family name that could be passed down to future generations as a family memento. Marty Silverman developed the idea for dispensing special *Operation Exodus tzedakah* boxes, and over 200,000 were distributed for the collection of smaller donations. The message of *Operation Exodus* was that every dollar counted and would play a role in bringing freedom to a Jew.

Educational programs were carried out in schools and camps to inform young people about the massive exodus and the resettlement needs. Rabbis addressed the needs of Jews from the former Soviet Union in their Sabbath sermons. National UJA developed special readings as inserts to the Passover *Haggadah,* to highlight the relationship between this exodus and those of times past. "Thank You America" speaker groups consisting of new *olim* traveled around the country speaking at schools, synagogues and Jewish community centers. UJA-Federation of New York sponsored "Israel 1990" and "Israel 1992" mega-missions, bringing over 1,500 people to Israel to witness and support the miracle of the exodus.

These and numerous other activities helped turn *Operation Exodus* into a highly personal event. Jews in the New York area were able to hear and read accounts of individual tribulations and personal courage, stories that inspired the entire Jewish community. Jews from all denominations and walks of life got involved in a united effort to raise money for the rescue and resettlement of Jews from the former Soviet Union. *Operation Exodus* became a household word in the New York Jewish community and around the country.

The national campaign, which officially lasted from January, 1990 to June 30, 1994, exceeded everyone's expectations. It raised nearly one billion dollars and generated more than a quarter million gifts. The Operation succeeded not only in rescuing and resettling vast numbers of Jews from abroad, but also in mobilizing and unifying the American Jewish community to an almost unprecedented degree.

## THE RESCUE:
### THE IMMENSITY OF THE EFFORT

The logistics of rescuing 500,000 Jews within such a brief timespan were enormous. The Soviet government did not permit departing Jews to take with them much money or possessions. Most could not pay for their plane tickets, and the diaspora Jewish community had to organize and oversee their entire journey, an undertaking in which the New York community played an important role. Donor dollars were used for plane fares and to enable the Jewish Agency For Israel to set up transit stations in Eastern Europe, particularly in Budapest and Bucharest for those going to Israel. For American-bound refugees, the American Jewish Joint Distribution Committee provided for their needs in centers located in towns surrounding Rome. The Hebrew Immigrant Aid Society (HIAS) helped the émigrés obtain proper documentation, visas and transportation. It was through monies provided by UJA-Federation of New York that JAFI, JDC and HIAS were able to furnish the necessary transportation and support.

With the large number of Jews passing through these centers weekly, the task of providing food and shelter was formidable. Determining where the Jews would emigrate to was another major problem. Early on, many Jews came to the United States, about half emigrating to New York City, to be reunited with their families but, as the numbers mushroomed and the U.S. revised its immigration policy, JAFI sent larger groups to Israel.

Despite the travails of leaving behind one's home and starting a new life, the Jews departing the former Soviet Union were encouraged by the new opportunities, and the vast majority began the resettlement process with an extremely positive attitude. Many attributed this to the support they received from the diaspora Jewish community, a phenomenon that greatly impressed them since there was no equivalent experience in the former Soviet Union. As soon as they were settled in Israel and, to a lesser degree, the United States, many brought over their families to join them. Some arranged for the emigration of more than 20 family members in a period of just a few years, a testament to the positive nature of their experience starting over in a new homeland.

## ETHIOPIA:
### AN EMERGENCY AIRLIFT

As Israel was absorbing ten to fifteen thousand Jews from the former Soviet Union each month during the peak years* of *Operation Exodus*, another dire need confronted the Jewish nation. The civil war in Ethiopia had created extreme hardship for its sizeable Jewish community, and the regime had begun to use the Jews as political pawns. Israel had been secretly negotiating with the government for the release of these people, and a last-minute agreement was reached for the Israeli military to evacuate the Jews. Because of the urgency of the situation, it had to be done within a matter of hours.

On May 24, 1991, Israel launched a massive secret airlift for the entire Ethiopian Jewish community. 250 buses carried the Ethiopians from the Israeli Embassy in Addis Ababa to the airfield, the site of

* The peak years of *Operation Exodus* were 1990-1992.

some 40 flights of the Israel Air Force and El Al planes. Within the space of 36 hours, 14,200 Jews were airlifted to freedom through *Operation Solomon.*

Having only one day's notice to prepare, a delegation from UJA-Federation of New York went to Israel to greet the planes and bear witness to this miraculous event. They arrived in time to see the last two planes land. The scene at Ben Gurion Airport was highly emotional, as Ethiopian family members found each other after many years of separation. While the Ethiopians were rejoicing, the Israeli people were demonstrating a tremendous spirit of volunteerism. The whole country geared up to receive these new *olim*, who were arriving from a society that was radically different from that of other immigrants who had settled in Israel. The Ethiopian Jews practiced Judaism as it was lived 2,500 years ago. In a strong show of support, Israelis brought clothing and goods, and schoolchildren gathered at the absorption centers to welcome the new arrivals and give them their first lesson in Hebrew.

## RESETTLEMENT: BEGINNING NEW LIVES

Even under the best of circumstances, emigration is accompanied by some degree of emotional trauma. The difficulties of adjusting to a new culture can be alleviated but not eliminated. In the case of Jews from the former Soviet Union, many aspects of Western society and economy were foreign to them. They were unprepared for such common challenges as job interviews or apartment hunting. Concepts such as credit were new to them. The need to make choices in health care and other aspects of daily life was also a novel experience.

Émigrés from the former Soviet Union experienced a decline in status, which made adjustment more difficult. In the past, their status was a function of their profession and education. Now, some trained professionals had to take jobs as unskilled workers. But they adapted rapidly, and many received training in new fields of work. Within a few years of their arrival in Israel, the unemployment rate for *olim* from the former Soviet Union was the same as for native Israelis: only about nine percent.

Despite their initial hardships, the new émigrés gathered tremendous strength from the Jewish community in Israel. Many began living Jewish lives for the first time. Under communism, most Jews had lost their connection to their Jewish roots; now, many began to observe the holidays and to integrate Jewish practices into their lives. When asked what made them leave the former Soviet Union, most would reply that they left for their children's futures, so they would have a better life and the freedom to live as Jews. The Jews that arrived in the United States and Israel were able to provide their children with an education in Jewish life, and many tell moving stories of their own return to Judaism through their children as a result of their new environment.

## NEW YORK:
### IMMIGRATION TO AMERICA

During the early waves of immigration that preceded *Operation Exodus*, many Jews from the former Soviet Union emigrated to the United States via New York City. In 1989, the United States government introduced a new immigration policy, limiting the Jews from the former Soviet Union who could apply for refugee status to those with families in the U.S., and emigration began to shift to Israel.

Those who came to New York were taken under the wing of the New York Association For New Americans (NYANA), the largest resettlement agency in the United States. NYANA — a UJA-Federation of New York beneficiary — provided temporary housing, a living allowance, English language classes, assistance in the job search, and social and mental health services. These immigrants could not have integrated as successfully without the help of the some 62 UJA-Federation of New York-supported agencies, which provided a full range of integrated services and expertise to meet the needs of this new population.

## ISRAEL:
### THE CHALLENGE OF RESETTLEMENT

The task of absorbing the surge of new immigrants from the former Soviet Union was a gargantuan one for Israel. During the peak years of 1990-92, Israel received in the neighborhood of 150,000 new *olim* a year. This influx of immigrants continued month after month, not slowing even during the Gulf War crisis in 1991, when Iraq fired scud missiles into Israel. On the first day of the war, Israel received 1,200 émigrés and, undaunted by the dangers of war, these new *olim* each received a gas mask at the airport after landing in Israel. To assist with the process of settling these Jews, Israel set up additional absorption centers. The Jewish Agency For Israel supervised the operation of these 42 centers, providing transportation and initial resettlement services.

Within approximately 24 hours of their arrival on Israeli soil, every new immigrant had a temporary home. They were placed in Hebrew language classes almost immediately, and provided with job counseling and retraining services. With 15,000 arrivals every month, each absorption center worked around the clock. The absorption effort was extremely well organized, and the ability of Israel to deal effectively with the movement of so many families is a remarkable chapter in the story of this exodus.

After 1991, Israel began direct absorption into communities throughout the country. Bypassing the absorption centers, immigrants received their own apartments right away in various cities and towns. Although the number of monthly arrivals began to decline slightly, the impact of all these new citizens was just beginning to be realized. Israel had mastered the initial steps of resettlement, but the process of absorbing these people into their economy was a more complex one: during the peak period, about 300 children entered Israel's school system each day; 100,000 new apartments needed to be built at a tremendous cost; 200,000 new jobs had to be created and a massive job retraining program established. Estimates of the total cost to Israel are as high as 40 billion dollars, a portion of which is being met by UJA-Federation funds.

The problems varied widely for resettling Jews from the former Soviet Union and those from Ethiopia. A majority of those coming from the former Soviet Union were trained professionals; a large percent were scientists and musicians. There is a limit, however, to the number of violinists or engineers any country can accommodate, and many of these professionals had to seek totally unrelated work. These new arrivals had little schooling in Jewish life, and Israel was often their first encounter with what it means to live as a Jew. The Ethiopians came from agrarian communities, and were ill-equipped to enter the advanced technological society of Israel. They had a rich religious tradition and identified strongly with their Jewish culture, but had difficulty in bridging 2,500 years of civilization.

The work of UJA-Federation, and the many positive resettlement stories in Israel, provided the inspiration needed to keep *Operation Exodus* strong and successful. UJA-Federation was able to turn this operation into an intrinsic part of Jewish institutional life. The growth and vitality of Israel has always been a central concern of the American Jewish community. Thus, American Jews, and New Yorkers in particular, were willing to extend themselves to such a great degree for the success of this operation.

## IMPACT:
### THE STRENGTHENING OF ISRAEL

There is no question that the long-term impact of *Operation Exodus* will advance the standing of Israel in the world community. The nearly 15 percent increase in Israel's population that *Operation Exodus* has so far brought is bolstering the country politically, culturally and ultimately economically. The tremendous influx of trained professionals has helped to put Israel on the cutting edge of technology. Some even foresee Israel in the next decade becoming one of the epicenters of the world, a place from which a whole new generation of innovations will emerge.

The mix of new arrivals from the former Soviet Union and Ethiopia is enriching the diversity of Israel's social fabric and invigorating its culture. Politically, the swelling of the population is also helping to increase Israel's security.

In the short-term, there will still be sacrifices as this sudden population growth strains Israel's economy — a strain that can largely be relieved by continued support from the Jewish community in the United States. Although officially *Operation Exodus* has ended as a separate fund-raising effort, the goal of continuing to raise money to rescue and resettle Jews from the former Soviet Union continues through UJA-Federation of New York's Annual Campaign. During *Operation Exodus'* four-year lifespan, over 500,000 refugees were helped to freedom. More than one million still remain in Russia and the neighboring republics; many of these people are just now beginning the process of *aliyah*.

The mass movement of Jews to Israel that is in progress is a bright moment in Jewish history. Centuries have passed with Jews being discriminated against and driven from one part of the world to another. This is a period of renewal, which Jews from the United States are helping to bring about with a remarkable spirit and extraordinary generosity. For the four years that comprised the *Operation Exodus* campaign, UJA-Federation led the way in uniting Jewish support. UJA-Federation will continue to sponsor the freedom of Jews from the former Soviet Union with the same fervor, until every Jew who chooses freedom in Israel is given that opportunity.

It is our hope that Jews throughout the New York area will continue to work with UJA-Federation for the ongoing success of this historic endeavor.

# THE

# PLIGHT:

## JEWS IN THE FORMER SOVIET UNION

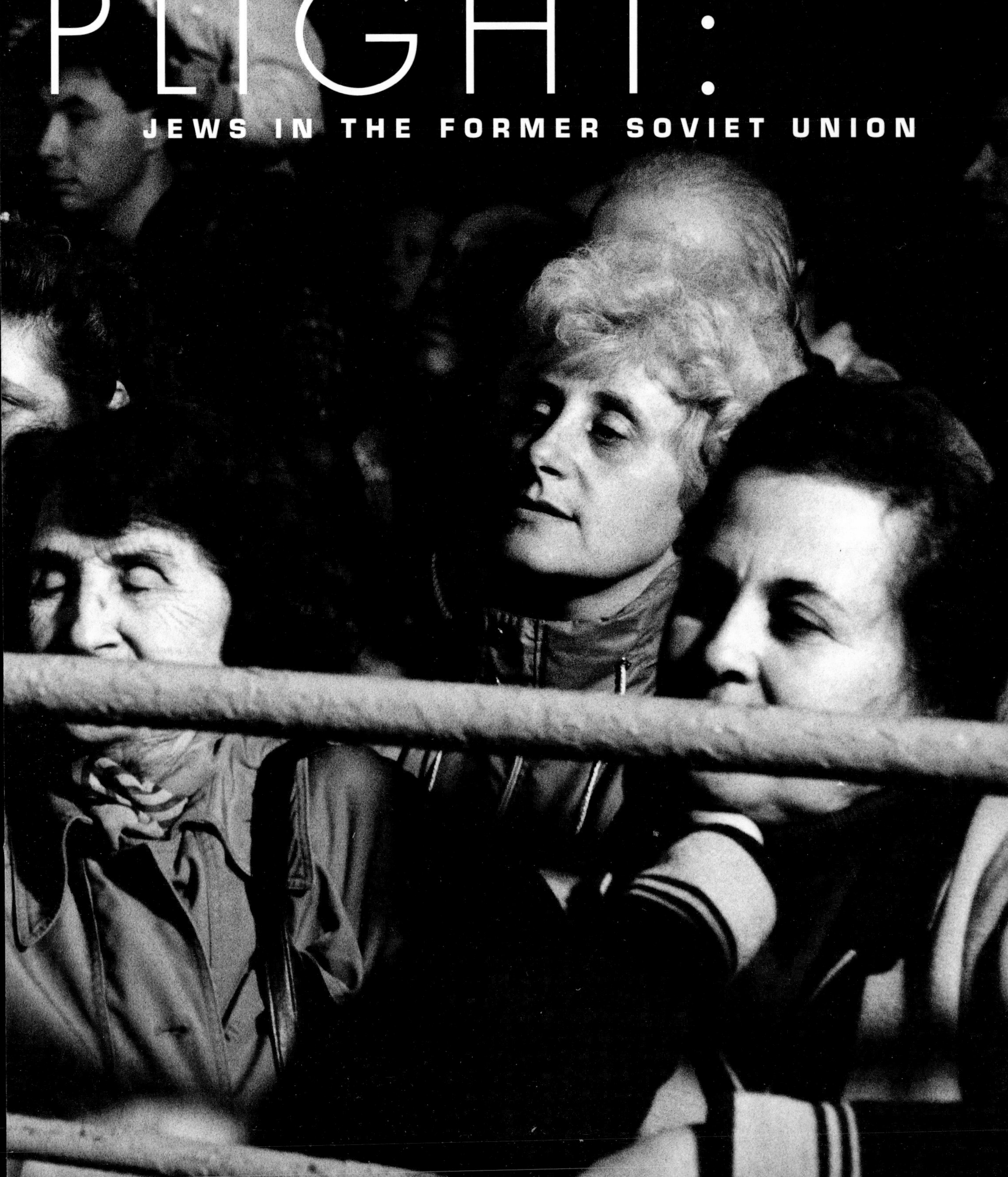

Anti-Semitism has been a subtle but pervasive force in Soviet society for many decades: Jews have not been admitted to certain universities; many could not advance in their careers; Jewish children have been made to feel as outsiders in their neighborhoods and schools; families have had to keep secret their Jewish heritage; Jewish cemeteries have been desecrated; and Jews have been required to list Hebrew as their nationality on their identification cards.

Previous page: In 1992, Jews from the former Soviet Union gathered at Babi Yar in the Ukraine to commemorate the 50th anniversary of the massacre of 200,000 Jews there. Continuing discrimination against Jews turned the commemoration into a particularly moving and symbolic event.

Opposite page: The Jewish elderly in the former Soviet Union are often left to poverty and despair. UJA-Federation of New York supports these elderly people through a variety of programs carried out by the JDC.

Above: Pamyat, a right wing anti-Semitic organization, demonstrates in Moscow. *Photo by Vlastimir Shone/Gamma Liason.*

LEONID A. WOLF

ХАБАД

Top left: A Jewish protester holding a picture of a refusenik at a demonstration in Moscow.

Bottom left: At the Babi Yar commemoration, past and present persecution is remembered.

Above: As the Soviet Union was unraveling, there was a liberalization of basic human rights. This picture shows a rabbi from New York City who has come to Russia to teach the Jews how to celebrate Jewish holidays.

Previous page: In the former Soviet Union, it was illegal to distribute Hebrew books. An elderly man looks after Jewish prayer books and scholarly texts that are stored in the attic of a synagogue.

Above: A deserted synagogue in St. Petersburg. Before the breakup of the former Soviet Union, only the elderly were permitted to attend synagogue. If other Jews went, the KGB would find out about it, and these individuals and their families would suffer.

Right: An elderly man in Riga seated outside a synagogue helps depict the lack of any active Jewish life in the former Soviet Union. The synagogues remained empty, even during holidays.

# THE

# CALL TO ACTION:

## NEW YORK RESPONDS

Previous page: A landmark event was Freedom Sunday on December 6, 1987, when New Yorkers were among the over 250,000 people who gathered in Washington, D.C. to meet Soviet leader Mikhail Gorbachev.

Above: The morning of the December 6, 1987, march on Washington, David Dinkins; Gary Ackerman; UJA-Federation leaders Peggy Tishman, Morton Kornreich, Judith Peck; and U.S. Attorney Rudolph Giuliani hold a press conference in New York to call attention to the plight of Soviet Jews.

Top right: Natan Sharansky.

Bottom right: Senator Patrick Moynihan, Cardinal O'Connor, Senator Alfonse D'Amato, Avital Sharansky (wife of Natan Sharansky) and New York State Attorney General Robert Abrams at a UJA-Federation-supported Solidarity Sunday rally for Soviet Jews.

**During the 1970s and 80s, UJA-Federation helped the New York Jewish community mobilize itself. Rallies were organized, badges and arm bracelets calling for the freedom of Soviet Jews were distributed, and letters from refuseniks were smuggled out of the former Soviet Union.**

Let All Our
People Go!

Left and above: The December 6, 1987, march on Washington.

Above: UJA-Federation supporters march in New York for the annual Salute to Israel Solidarity Parade holding large *tzedakah* boxes, which were used to raise money for *Operation Exodus*. The use of *tzedakah* boxes was one of the ways UJA-Federation engaged widespread community support. *Photograph by Alan Rosenberg.*

Far right: A Jewish mother in New York stands before a picture of her daughter, who is unable to get out of the former Soviet Union. Jews unable to leave were often referred to as "prisoners of *Zion*."

Right: A rally in New York in support of Soviet Jews.

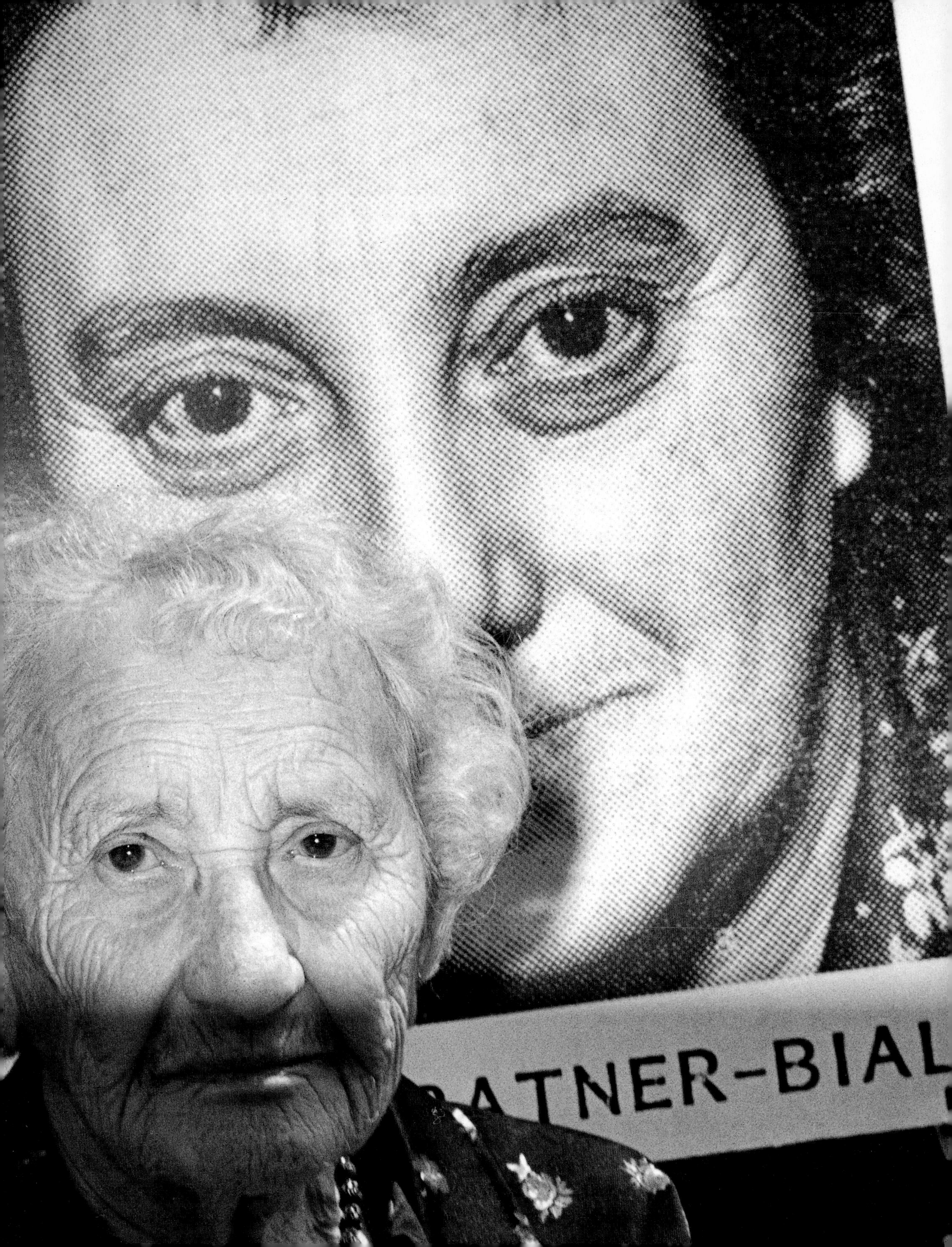
ATNER-BIAL

# THE

# FLIGHT:
## LEAVING THE FORMER SOVIET UNION

**The environment in the former Soviet Union became so unsettling for Jews that when Gorbachev opened the doors to emigration in 1989-1990, Jews responded with a fervor, flocking in droves to the train stations and airports of Moscow.**

Previous page: Jews on a train departing for Israel from Kishinev, the capital of the Republic of Moldavia, wave goodbye to those they are leaving behind.

Opposite page: Jews leave for Israel from a train station in Kishinev. They are traveling to Israel via Bucharest, Rumania.

Above: A young man sits on the track at the train station in Kishinev. His friend has just departed for Israel. He has applied for an emigration visa but has not received it.

МЕСТ-36

Families and friends saying goodbye at the train station in Moldavia. Such scenes were highly emotional as families left many loved ones behind. Those staying in the former Soviet Union had no way of knowing when they would be granted visas to leave. Over time, through money raised by *Operation Exodus*, many were able to bring family members to Israel or the United States.

EL AL אל על

Previous page: A UJA-Federation-sponsored Freedom Flight lands at Ben Gurion Airport, Jerusalem. For many Jews living in the United States, one of the most dramatic moments of the whole *Operation Exodus* effort was the sight of Jews from the former Soviet Union descending the stairway of the Freedom Flight they had sponsored.

Left and below: Jews from the former Soviet Union arrive at Ben Gurion Airport. Many New Yorkers went to Israel to greet first-hand the new immigrants whose freedom they had sponsored.

Above and right: Jews from the former Soviet Union receive gas masks as they arrive in Israel during the Gulf War. Even as scud missiles were falling on Israel, they continued to arrive in large numbers. On the first day of the war, Israel received 1,200 new émigrés.

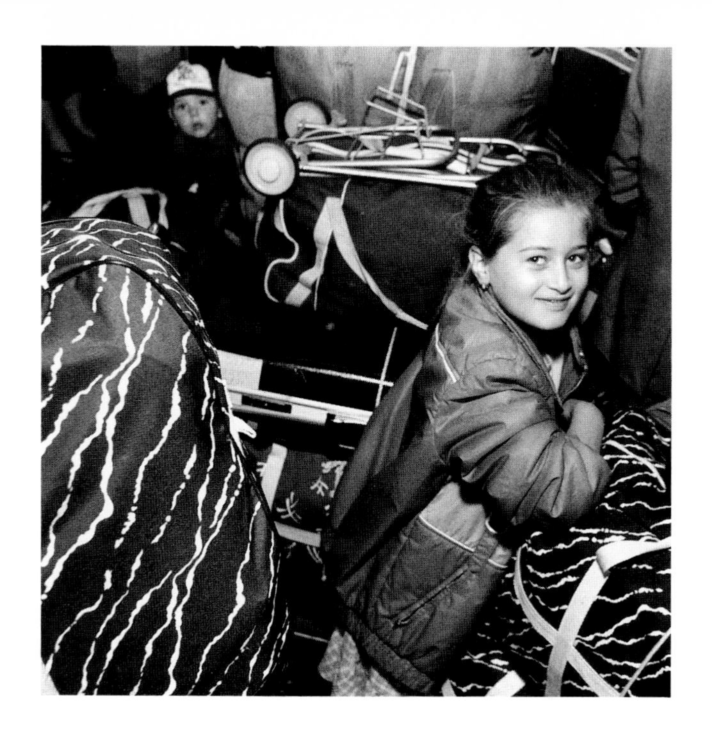

Above: At Ben Gurion Airport, Jews from the former Soviet Union wait for their papers to be processed.

Right: During the *Operation Exodus* Campaign, the first plane of Soviet Jews arrives at John F. Kennedy International Airport in New York City.

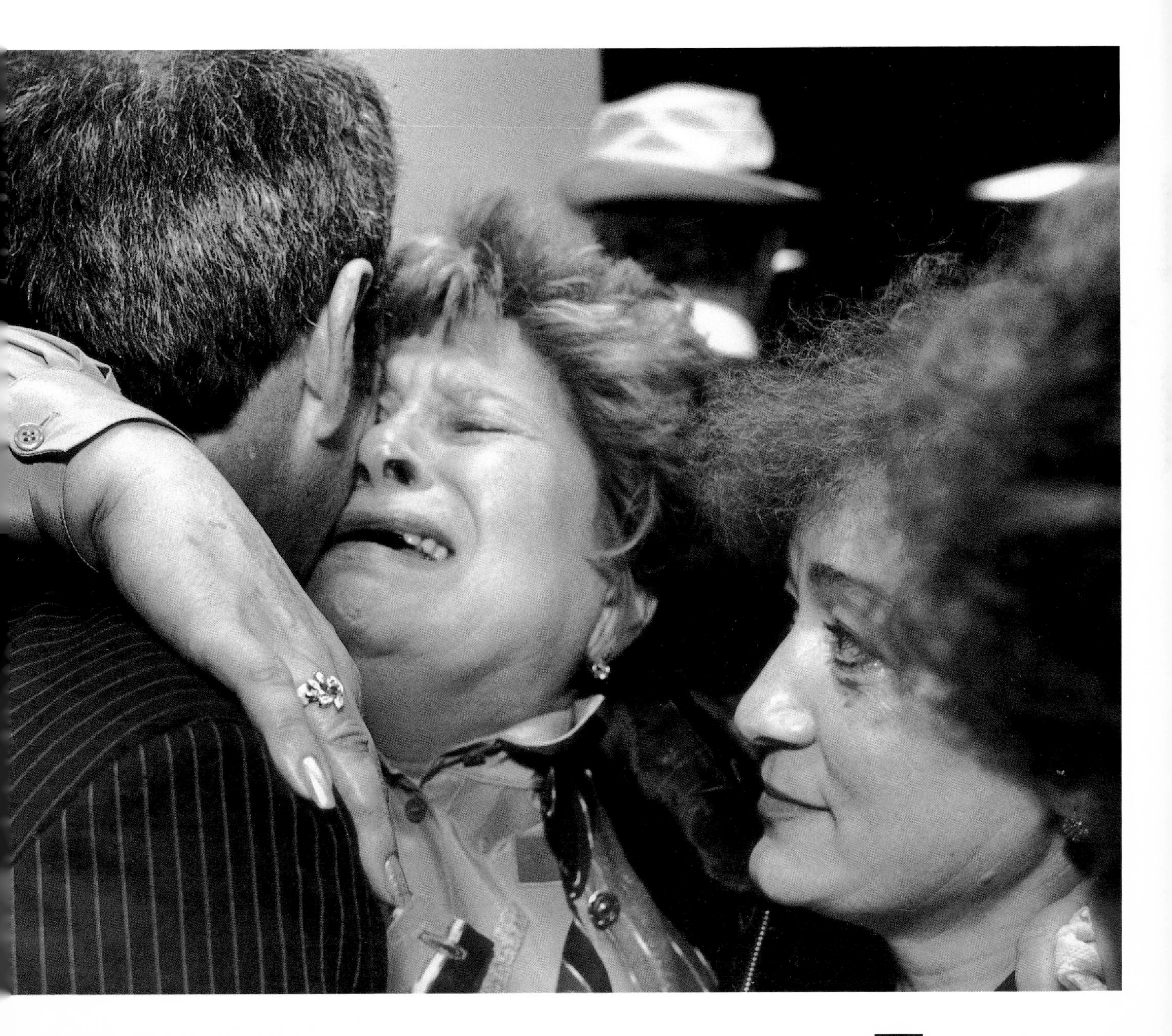

# THE FLIGHT:

## LEAVING ETHIOPIA

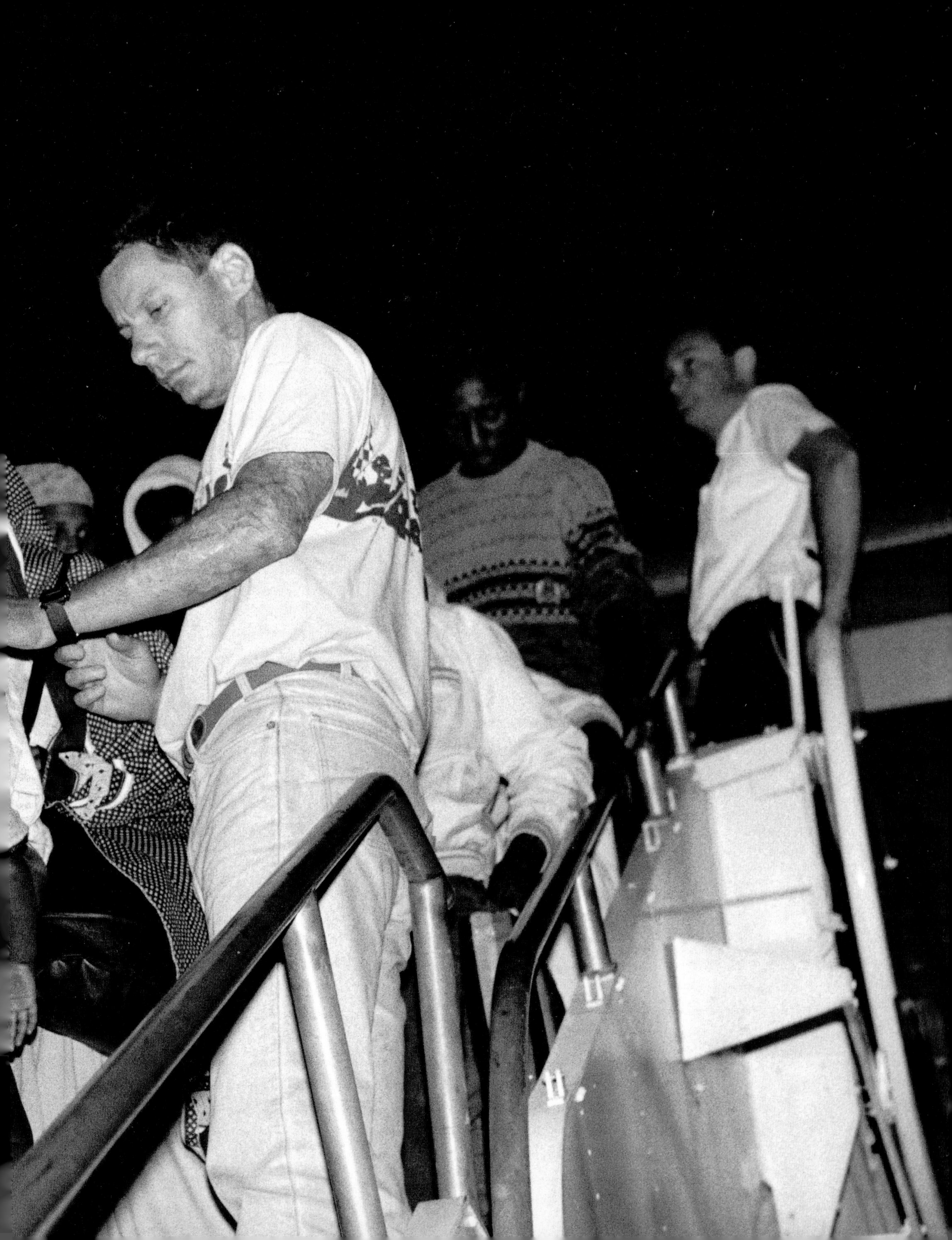

**On May 24, 1991, Israel launched a massive secret airlift for the entire Ethiopian Jewish community: 250 buses carried the Ethiopians from the Israeli Embassy in Addis Ababa to the airfield, the site of some 40 sorties of the Israel Air Force and El Al planes. Within the space of 36 hours, 14,200 Jews were airlifted to freedom through *Operation Solomon*, which was incorporated into the *Operation Exodus* Campaign.**

Previous page: An Israeli assists the Ethiopians as they arrive in Israel.

Left: An Ethiopian man carries his mother on his back after landing in Israel.

Above: A young Ethiopian arrives in Israel. Many Ethiopian families had been separated for years, as some family members had managed to escape to Israel before this mass exodus. *Operation Solomon* reunited many families.

Right: One of the seven babies born on the planes that carried the Ethiopians from Addis Ababa to Israel.

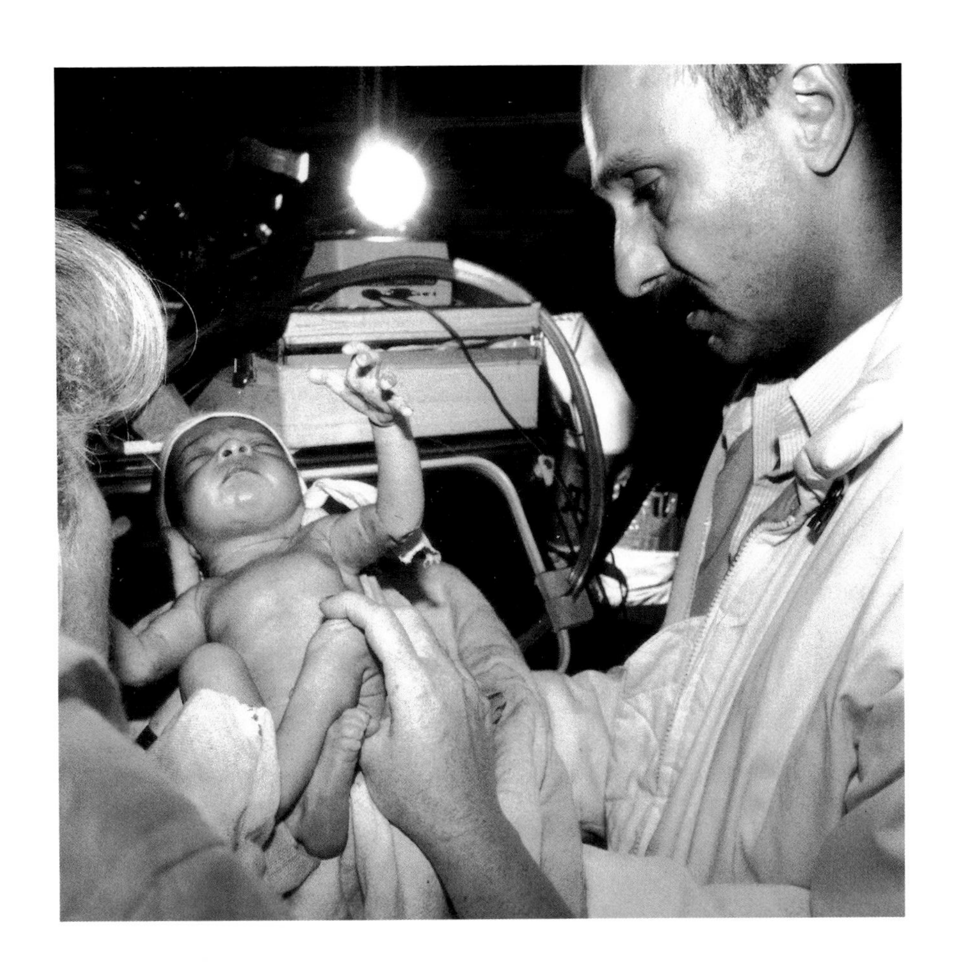

Left: An Israeli soldier, who is Ethiopian, carries an Ethiopian child from the plane.

Right: Ethiopian families arrive in Israel. The Hercules plane from which they are descending is an Israeli army plane used for transport. To accommodate the large number of people, the seats were taken out of the plane so that people could line the floor space, filling the entire plane.

A NEW

# LIFE:

## RESETTLING IN ISRAEL

**Even under the best of circumstances, emigration is accompanied by some degree of emotional trauma. Despite their initial hardships, the new émigrés gathered tremendous strength from the Jewish community in Israel and the United States. Many began living Jewish lives for the first time.**

Previous page: Some 1,000 New Yorkers went to Israel on the UJA-Federation-sponsored "Israel 1990" mega-mission to witness the miracle of *Operation Exodus*. When they greeted a planeload of arriving Jews from the former Soviet Union, one elderly émigré man kissed the hand of a mission participant in gratitude for helping to make his freedom possible.

Left: Children in a pre-school class at an absorption center in Israel. These new émigrés are learning how to celebrate the Sabbath.

Right and below: In Jerusalem, caravans of mobile homes were brought in to accommodate the new *olim*. These homes were set up after the absorption centers became full.

Through a variety of UJA-Federation supported programs, the new immigrants are helped to make the transition to a new life in Israel.

Opposite page bottom: With UJA-Federation support, an American student from New York is working as a volunteer to teach Hebrew to young Ethiopians.

Opposite page top: Children from the former Soviet Union and Ethiopia learn Hebrew in a class at an absorption center.

Left: A woman from the former Soviet Union with her granddaughter discovers the diversity of foods in an Israeli supermarket.

Below: Israeli women bring clothes to Ethiopians at a mobile home settlement in the Negev.

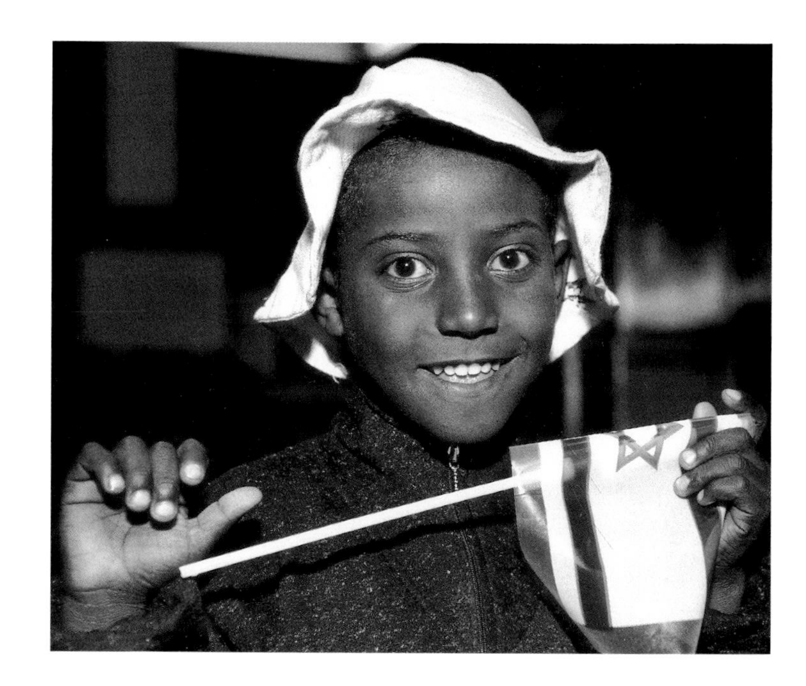

ילד
ילדים
Don't
Don't
Just

Opposite page left: With UJA-Federation support, children from the former Soviet Union learn Hebrew at a school in Brooklyn.

Opposite page right: Ethiopian children at school in Israel learn about Jewish holidays.

This page: Children from the former Soviet Union and Ethiopia in Israel. Many immigrants from the former Soviet Union decided to leave their country so their children could have a better life and have the opportunity to live as Jews. In Israel, these children quickly adapt to Israeli culture.

victory
SPORTSHOES
& FASHION
THE BRAND
FOR WINNERS

Left: "Israel 1990" participants gather on the tarmac of Ben Gurion Airport to welcome Jews from the former Soviet Union as they step off the plane and onto Israeli soil. The "Israel 1990" mission was the largest single delegation of New Yorkers ever to visit Israel at one time.

Above: On the right is David Sacks, then UJA-Federation President, as he participated in greeting the new *olim* on the 1990 mega-mission to Israel.

Left and above: Scenes from Brighton Beach, a hub of Russian Jewish life in New York City. 62 UJA-Federation-sponsored agencies provided these and other immigrants from the former Soviet Union with the services and financial support they needed to begin a new life.

# IMPACT:

## THE STRENGTHENING OF ISRAEL

The nearly 15 percent increase in Israel's population that *Operation Exodus* has so far brought is bolstering the country politically, culturally and ultimately economically. The tremendous influx of trained professionals already has put Israel on the cutting edge of technology. Some even foresee Israel in the next decade becoming one of the epicenters of the world, a place from which a whole new generation of innovations will emerge.

Previous page: A man from the former Soviet Union works at an industrial site in Israel.

Left: A new émigré works in a print shop.

Below: An immigrant at his job as an engineer. Many of these highly skilled professionals from the former Soviet Union were able to be placed in jobs for which they were trained. Others had to seek retraining through special programs.

Above: A Russian émigré working at a job with metals.

Right: A newly retrained immigrant works with technical equipment in Israel.

Below: Scientists from the former Soviet Union at a lab in Jerusalem.

Far left: A violinist from the former Soviet Union performs with an orchestra in Israel.

Top left: An artist from the former Soviet Union works at her studio in Israel.

Left: Jews from Ethiopia and the former Soviet Union learn construction at a special training program near Jerusalem.

Above: A physician from the former Soviet Union engaged in research at a lab in Israel.

Left: A Soviet Jew at work in a tomato greenhouse in the Negev.

Above: One of the new *olim* cares for turkeys on a farm in a kibbutz in northern Israel.

Left: A family from the former Soviet Union in front of their new home at an apartment complex in Jerusalem.

Right: A family from Ethiopia stands before new apartments in Jerusalem.

**During *Operation Exodus'* four-year lifespan, over 500,000 refugees were helped to freedom. More than one million still remain in Russia and its neighboring republics. Many of these people are just now beginning the process of *aliyah*. This mass movement of Jews that is in progress is a bright moment in Jewish history. It is a period of renewal for Israel and for Jews around the world.**

## UJA-FEDERATION OF NEW YORK

Officers Governing During Operation Exodus
(March 15, 1990 - June 30, 1994)

**Chairman, Board of Directors**

Joseph Gurwin, 1988 - 1991
Irwin Hochberg, 1991 - 1994

**President**

David G. Sacks, 1989 - 1992
Alan S. Jaffe, 1992 - 1995

**Executive Vice President**

Stephen D. Solender

**General Chairman, Campaign**

Larry A. Silverstein, 1990
Harvey Schulweis, 1991
Alvin H. Einbender, 1992
James S. Tisch, 1993 - 1994

**Chairman, Domestic Affairs Division**

Alan S. Jaffe, 1989 - 1992
Louise B. Greilsheimer, 1992 - 1994

**Chairman, Overseas Affairs Division**

Irwin Hochberg, 1988 - 1991
Alan Batkin, 1991 - 1993
Herbert Kronish, 1993 - 1994

**Treasurer**

Philip A. Laskawy, 1990 - 1993
Alan S. Bernikow, 1993 - 1994

**Secretary**

Myrtle Hirsch*, 1990
Selma Shavitz, 1991 - 1994

**Chief Operating Officer, Financial Resources**

Adam B. Kahan

**Chief Operating Officer, Program Services**

Jeffrey R. Solomon

**deceased*

## OPERATION EXODUS COMMITTEE

**Chairman**
Peter W. May

**Co-Chairman**
Alexander E. Fisher

**Honorary Chairmen**
William Rosenwald
Jack D. Weiler

**Honorary Members**
Edgar M. Bronfman
Laurence A. Tisch

**Committee Members**
Andrea A. Aaron
Philip S. Altheim
Sanford Antignas
Bruce Berger
Robert S. Boas*
Ludwig Bravmann
Anni Bruss
Jerry L. Cohen
Lawrence J. Cohen
Mel Dubin
Alvin H. Einbender
Robert W. Fischer
Patrice Fragin
Meryl Gallatin
David Gordon
Irwin Hochberg
Dr. Albert Hornblass
Leon Kalvaria
Ludmila Kislin
Paul J. Konigsberg
Paul Kronish
Alice L. Kulick
Nathan Low
Burton J. Manning
Stephen Neuburger
Irving Schneider
Harvey Schulweis
Jodi J. Schwartz
Daniel S. Shapiro
Larry A. Silverstein
Harriet G. Sloane
Jeffrey J. Steiner
Michael Steinhardt
Lawrence M. Stern
Andrew M. Sternlieb
Andrew H. Tisch
Peggy Tishman
Elizabeth R. Varet
Lawrence Wajnberg
Sarah B. Weinstein
Neil Wyler

**deceased*

## OPERATION EXODUS STAFF

**Executive Director**
Kenneth J. Gabel, 1989 - 1991

**Director**
Stephen G. Doochin, 1991 - 1994

**Assistant Directors**
David Bellin, 1990 - 1992
Felice Kobylanski, 1990
Nanette Ross, 1991 - 1994

**Roll of Honor Team**
Project Manager
Ron Brien

Rachel Blumkin
Bea DeVito
Linda Emanuel
Angela Gonzalez
Robert Gurmankin
Carmen Hernandez
Jim Julier
Esther Kaminoff
Nan Leibowitz
Michael LoSardo
Ricki Lubov
Cynthia Schupf
Mamie Sheppeard
Linda Simon
Loren Spivack

OPERATION
EXODUS
1990-1994

# OPERATION EXODUS
## ROLL OF HONOR

**This Roll of Honor recognizes donors who contributed more than $1,000 to UJA-Federation of New York's Operation Exodus Campaign as of October 1, 1994, and recites the names of those who agreed to be listed as such through written authorization received by December 23, 1994. Operation Exodus donors who gave more than $1,000 who chose not to be included in this Roll of Honor, or whose written response was never received or received after December 23, 1994, are not listed in this Roll of Honor.**

**This book honors all those donors who supported Operation Exodus — whether or not their names appear below — and we are eternally grateful for their support.**

### $5,000,000 and Over
Edgar M. Bronfman
The Rudin Family
Helen and Irving Schneider

### $1,000,000 and Over
Anonymous
Louis and Anne Abrons
Foundation, Inc.
The Baron De Hirsch Fund
The Forchheimer Foundation
Kathy and Alan Greenberg
Ludwig and Erica Jesselson
Ruth and Leonard Litwin
Leni and Peter May
The Milstein Family Foundation
Samuel I. Newhouse
Foundation, Inc.
Claudia and Nelson Peltz
Frederick, Daniel and Elihu Rose
The William Rosenwald Family
S. H. and Helen R. Scheuer
Family Foundation
The Skirball Foundation,
Morris H. Bergreen, President
The Tisch Families
Wachtell, Lipton, Rosen & Katz
Jack D. Weiler

### $500,000 and Over
Anonymous
Simon A. Bond
The Brookdale Foundation Group
Alfred and Gail Engelberg
Shirley and Milton Gralla
Mr. and Mrs. Maurice R. Greenberg
J. Gurwin Foundation, Inc.
Raphael Recanati
The Joseph E. and
Norma G. Saul Foundation, Inc.
Dianne and David Stern
Weil, Gotshal and Manges
Elaine and Jim Wolfensohn

### $250,000 and Over
Anonymous
Mr. and Mrs. Leon Ajces
Barbara and Philip Altheim
Diane and Arthur Belfer
Robert and Renee Belfer
David Berg, Esq.
Robert S. Boas*
Barbara and Joel Boyarsky
Lotte and Ludwig Bravmann
Mr. and Mrs. Alvin H. Einbender
Ernst & Young
Stephen and Barbara Friedman
Horace W. Goldsmith Foundation
Jay and Diane Goldsmith
David and Ruth Gottesman
Stella and Charles Guttman
Foundation, Inc.
Stephen and Eleanor Hammerman
Kamber Management, Inc.,
Mr. and Mrs. Stanley H. Levy
Mr. and Mrs. Steven M. Levy
Mr. and Mrs. Peter B. Levy
Helen and Martin Kimmel
Ludmila and Semyon Kislin
Jerome Kohlberg, Jr.
H. Thomas and Evelyn Langbert
Barbara and Morris Levinson
William and Helen Mazer
Foundation, Inc.
Henry and Lucy Moses Fund, Inc.
Geri and Lester Pollack
Laura and John Pomerantz
Judith and Burton Resnick
Carol and Harvey Schulweis
Marvin C. Schwartz
Larry A. Silverstein
Sheldon H. Solow
Mr. and Mrs. Meyer Steinberg
Jeffrey Steiner Family
Judy and Michael Steinhardt
Sterling Equities, Inc.,
Mr. Saul B. Katz
Mr. Fred Wilpon
Mr. Michael Katz
Mr. Richard A. Wilpon
Barbara and Roy Zuckerberg

### $100,000 and Over
Anonymous
Mrs. Susan Aberbach
Andrew, James and
Mitchell Benerofe
Froma Benerofe
Meyer and Pat Berman
Joseph and Ralph Bernstein
Zella and Jack E. Bulter Foundation
Robert Carmel
Patricia and James Cayne
Michael J. Chasanoff
Adrianne and Jerry L. Cohen
Mr. and Mrs. Albert B. Cohen
J. Morton Davis
Eleanor and Mel Dubin
Edith and Henry Everett
Patrice and Gary Fragin
Judge Jacob D. and
Shirley Fuchsberg
Meryl and Ronald L. Gallatin
Alice and Nathan Gantcher
The David Geffen Foundation
Lila Gimprich
Mr. and Mrs. Eugen Gluck
Jerome Gottesman
Eugene and Emily Grant
Hana Green
Lawrence and Roslyn Greenfield
Aaron Gural
Evelyn and Sol Henkind
Ronnie and Samuel J. Heyman
Jonathan Ilany
Bernice and Sidney Jacobson
John and Fred Klingenstein
Murray Koppelman
Morton A. Kornreich
Mr. and Mrs. Henry R. Kravis
Alice L. Kulick
The Leff Family, Morgan and
Marjorie Miller
Harold I. Leviton
Martin R. Lewis
David and Lilly Lieb
Robert K. Lifton
Ellen and Richie Markowitz
Robert and Wendy Meister
Meshedi Community, Congregation
Shaarei Tova, Kew Gardens
The Mishkin Family
Morton and Carole
Olshan Foundation
Irene and Murray Pergament
Mr. Bertram Podell
Alan H. and Lillian P. Posner
Ingeborg and Ira Leon Rennert
Jack and Pearl Resnick Foundation
Howard and Amy Rubenstein
Helena Rubinstein Foundation
Bernice and Cecil Rudnick
Irving and Geraldine Schaffer
Albert and Claire Schussler
Joan and Jerry Serchuck
Mr. and Mrs. Jesse S. Siegel
Saul Singer
Mr. and Mrs. Alan B. Slifka
Harriet G. Sloane
Jerry I. Speyer
Gerald and Ronda Starr
Lynne and Michael L. Tarnopol
Peggy and Alan Tishman
Mr. and Mrs. William Ungar
Muriel and Howard Weingrow
Shoshanna and David A. Wingate
William and Lisa Wishnick
The Zale Foundation,
Gloria and Jerry Landsberg
Carol and David Zale
Claudia and Stanley Zale
Karen and Steven Seltzer
Renate and Martin Zimet

### $50,000 and Over
Anonymous
Lorraine and Richard Abramson
Anchin, Block and Anchin
Atran Foundation, Inc.
Jane and Alan Batkin
Captain and Mrs. Leo V. Berger
Phyllis and Irving Bernstein
Estate of Paula Better
Jerry and Evelyn Bishop
Mr. and Mrs. Stanley M. Bogen
Charles R. Borrok

*deceased

Hubert J. Brandt
Louise and David Braver
Ann L. and Lawrence B. Buttenwieser
The Cannold Family Foundation
Carol and Geoffrey Chinn
Irving and Ruth Claremon
Mr. and Mrs. Milton L. Cohen
Robert De Rothschild
Elyssa and Mark Dickstein
Laura and Benjamin Duhl
Stuart and Lynn Epstein
Harold and Isabel Feld
Symon and Eda Ferman
Claudette and Manny Fink
Maria and Joel Finkle
Alexander and Enid Fisher
Mr. and Mrs. Jerome Fisher
Marjorie and Albert Fortinsky
Mr. and Mrs. Alan Fortunoff
Frederick Frank
Mr. and Mrs. Roland A. E. Franklin
Harold and Sylvia N. Friedman
Ira M. Friedman
Fuchsberg and Fuchsberg
The Moses Ginsberg Family Foundation, Calmon J. Ginsberg
Sol and Rose Ginsburg Foundation, Sam and Joan Ginsburg Martin and Irene Ginsburg
Marilyn and Allen Glick
Bradley and Sunny Y. Goldberg
John and Suzanne Golden
Mr. and Mrs. Arnold Goldstein
Cynthia and Bennett Golub
Edward S. Gordon Company, Inc.
David and Bernice Gotlieb
Fanya Gottesfeld-Heller
Helaine and Fred Gould
The Green Fund, Inc.
Myrna and Herbert Greissman
Dr. Robert and Brenda Hamby
Saul B. Hamond
Richard and Karen Harriton
Sylvia Hassenfeld
Ruth and Stephen Hendel
Rhoda R. Herrick
Edythe and George Heyman
David and Rochelle Hirsch
Rita and Irwin Hochberg
Mrs. Muriel Horowitz
Liz and Alan Jaffe
Charlotte and Jules Joskow
Eli and Lila Kalimian
Alice and Allan Kaplan
Kaye Insurance Associates, L. P.
Evelyn B. Kenvin
Peter and Eva Kessner
Koeppel Martone Leistman & Herman
Meyer and Ellen Koplow
Lynn Korda Kroll
Lillian and Ira N. Langsan Foundation
Elsie and Leon Levy
J. S. Liebowitz Foundation, Inc.
Arthur L. Liman
Armand and Jean Lindenbaum
Mr. and Mrs. John L. Loeb, Sr.
Dedee and Steve Lovell
Saul H. Magram
Vivian and Edward Merrin
Meshedi Jewish Community of Great Neck
Martin and Joan Messinger
Saul Miller, Bernard Miller and Dr. George Miller
Michael and Cheryl Minikes
Ann and Bert Moreida
Moroze Sherman Gordon & Gordon, Issac and Judith Sherman Nahum and Barbara Gordon David and Karen Gordon
The Jean and Albert Nerken Foundation
Mr. and Mrs. William Overman
Sally and Henry Pearce
Sassoon and Marjorie Peress
Claire and Sidney Perlman, Samuel Field Family Foundation
Yvonne and Leslie Pollack
Samuel Posner
Arnold and Irene Rabinor
Jacques and Alina Roisen
Doris and Edward Rosenthal
Susan and Jon Rotenstreich
David and Naomi Sacks
Jane Dresner Sadaka and Ned Sadaka
Jack and Anita Saltz
Suki and Herman S. Sandler
Michael Saperstein
Samuel Schaeffler
Alfred and Shirley Schechter
Irwin Schneiderman
Irwin Schnurmacher
Jack and Margo Schwartz
Jeffrey and Wendy Schwarz
Ellen S. and Daniel S. Shapiro
Ruth and Irwin Shapiro
David and Jean Shechet
The Shubert Foundation
Ann and Herb Siegel
William and Sylvia Silberstein
Julius Silver, Esq.
Harvey and Karen Silverman
Nell and Herb Singer
Joseph and Marcy Sirulnick
Marian and Merrill Skeist
Warren J. Spector
Joseph F. Stein Foundation, Inc.
Mr. and Mrs. Robert Steinberg
Jeffrey M. Stern and Susan K. Stern
Mr. and Mrs. Steven E. Stern
Joan H. Strausberg
The Tilles Family
Daniel R. Tishman
Glen and Lynn Tobias
Esther and Ted Treitel
The Tsesarsky Family
Waldbaum's Supermarket Company
Sarah and Robert Wax
Terri and Evan Wein
Elaine and Norman Winik
Steven and Joyce Wolitzer
Maxine and Samuel Zinder

## $25,000 and Over

Anonymous
Samuel Aaron, Inc.
Carmela and Milton Ackman
Mr. and Mrs. Lawrence D. Ackman
Joseph S. Allerhand
Marilyn Marcus Alper
Nathan S. Ancell
Edith Marks Baldinger
Tilly Baron
Harry and Lore Bauer
Jayne and Harvey Beker
Mimi and Burton Belsky
Bruce and Barbara Berger
Charles M. and Jane P. Berger
Rochelle and Edward Berkowitz
Elaine and Arthur H. Bienenstock
Sylvia and Joseph Binder
Martin and Rena Blackman
Kate Blaser and Frederick S. Blaser
Devorah and Mel Bleiberg
Peter Bloom and Jane Greenfield
Frances Brandt
Mrs. Ann Loeb Bronfman
Fred and Hansi Browning
Al and Belle Bukiet
The Jacob Burns Foundation, Inc.
Mrs. Marilyn Butler
Mr. and Mrs. Morton Certilman
Phyllis and Leon Charash
Mr. and Mrs. Wallace Chavkin
Abe M. and Geri Cohen Foundation
Sherman and Gloria Cohen
Marcia and Ronald S. Cooper
Mr. and Mrs. Sol Neil Corbin
Mr. and Mrs. Joseph F. Cullman, 3rd
Judith and Richard Darsky
DDK & Company, Allen R. Dorkin David C. Drescher Edward M. Kaplan Richard Klinghoffer Jeffrey E. Zukoff Stewart J. Langhaus
Esther and Daniel Diamond
Mr. and Mrs. Charles M. Diker
Elisabeth and Alan Doft
Bunny and B. J. Douek
Leon and Lea Eisenberg
Leslie and David Fastenberg
Susan and Leonard Feinstein
Esther and Harvey Felsen
Alan and Susan Finkelstein
David and Judy Fleischer
Dr. Francis Foldes
Mildred and Gene Forrell
Saradee and Stanley Fortgang
Mr. and Mrs. Steven M. Friedman
Miriam Loewy Friend
Pauline and Joseph Frisch
E. and S. Fuchsberg
Alice Jarcho and Thomas Gallagher
Linda and David Garrett
Stuart and Micki Gilbert
Mr. and Mrs. Daniel Glassman
Drs. Felix and Miriam Glaubach
Jean Gluck
Mr. and Mrs. Steven Gluckstern
Billie and Martin Gold
Bernard Goldberg
Jocelyn and Robert S. Goldman
Steven and Carol Goldschein
Nathan and Louise Goldsmith Foundation
Michael Goldstein
Wendy and Mark N. Goldstein
Michael and Lola Goodstein
Gloria and Jesse Gottlieb
Mr. and Mrs. Jules A. Gottlieb
Mr. and Mrs. Robert Granovsky
Charlotte and Morris L. Green
Phyllis and Murray H. Greenspan
Edward and Edith Greenwald
Max Grill
Mr. and Mrs. Gedalio Grinberg
Mr. and Mrs. Mike Havkins
Michael and Sandy Hecht
Ellen and David S. Hirsch
Joyce and Richard Hirsch
Stephen M. Hoffman, Stewart F. Hoffman
Robert and Fern Hurst
Drs. Roger A. and Susan S. Hyman
Robert L. Israeloff
Dr. and Mrs. Julius Jacobson
Abi and Mona Kalimian
Daniel S. Kampel
Kanofsky Family
Myra F. Kaplan
Trudy and Howard Kaplan
Susan and Richard Katcher
Mr. and Mrs. Jerome L. Katz
Judy and Earle W. Kazis
Dr. and Mrs. Charles D. Kelman
Peter and Eva Kessner
Alfred D. and E. Temma Kingsley
Ludwig Klauber
Milo and Bertha Kleinberg
Ruth and Lawrence Kobrin
Paul J. Konigsberg, Robert I. Konigsberg and Steven Mendelow
Dale and Stephen Kramer

Herbert and Doris Kronish
Paul Kronish
Ann and Ben Kwitman
Betsy and Donald Landis
Barbara and Richard S. Lane
Philip and Patricia Laskawy
Helen and Jack Lazar Foundation
Betty and John Levin
Ezra and Batya Levin
Karen and Joseph Levine
Kathleen and Jeffrey Lewis
Cheryl and Glen Lewy
Richard and Annie Linhart
Yocheved and Donald Liss
Shumer Lonoff
Edward and Hannah Low
Susan and Edwin Malloy
Gladys and Matthew J. Maryles and Family
Sol Matsil
Mr. and Mrs. Hermann Merkin
Joan and Leon Meyers
Ellen R. Dunkin and Joseph Michaeli
Mr. and Mrs. Theodore N. Mirvis
Jack and Julie Moersel
Gerald and Ruth Monter
Dr. Frank Moore's Family
Carole and Harold Moskowitz
Joshua Nash
Belle and Murray L. Nathan
Gabriel Nechamkin
Florence and Henry K. Neidich
The Neuburger Family
North Shore Sephardic Synagogue
Barry and Barbara Novick
Mrs. Beryl F. Oppenheimer
Ronald F. Ostrow
Fritzi and Herbert Owens
Ruth and Sam Perelson
Wilma and Louis Perlman
Mr. and Mrs. Nathan M. Perlmutter
Charles and Elaine Petschek
Kenneth and Bettina Plevan
Propp Family
Mr. and Mrs. Donald Rabinovitch
Mr. Asriel Rackow
Nancy and Roy R. Raizen
Phyllis and Douglas Rimsky
Andrew Rodman and Lisa Rodman
Nina and Allan Rodolitz
George and Pamela Rohr
Rona and Steven Z. Rones
Martin and Joan Rosen
Sandy and Walter Rosen
Irving M. Rosenbaum
Joseph B. Rosenblatt, The Rosenblatt Family Group
Martin Rosenman
Salzhauer Family
Phyllis and Stanley Sanders
Philip Schatten
Jerry Schellenberg
Brenda and Jonathan Scher
Lynn and Philip M. Schlussel
Lynn Schneider
Jodi J. Schwartz
Miriam and Nathan Schwartz
Barbara and Paul Seidenberg
Searle and Cynthia Selmon
Yosef, Shahrokh, Farzad Shahery
Elaine and Harold Shames
Joseph and Nina Shenker
Bernice and Aaron A. Sherman
Sidney and Marjorie Silberman
Klara Silverstein
The Silverweed Foundation
Sylvia and Donald Simon
Doris and Melvin Sirow
Stephen I. Soble
Beverly Sommer
Dr. and Mrs. Edward Soufer and Family
Mr. and Mrs. Bernard Stein
Andrew M. Sternlieb
Claire and Edward Stiepleman
Myron Stone
The Strausman Family
Thomas W. Strauss
Harriet and Marc Suvall
Mrs. Shelby Tauber
Judy and Warren Tenney
Leonard and Anne Thun
Diane and Gerald Tohn
Debra and David Trachtenberg
Mr. and Mrs. William B. Troy
Mr. and Mrs. Fred Tryfus
Bella and Israel Unterberg Foundation
Jill and Daniel Wallen
James L. Weinberg
Mr. and Mrs. Robert F. Weinberg
Dr. Miklos and Eva Weinberger
The Isak and Rose Weinman Foundation, Inc.
Kenneth and Carol Weiser
Alice and Louis Weiss
Selma and Daniel Weiss
Arlene Wittels
Milton Wittels
Sue and Albert Wojnilower
Jacob J. Worenklein
Nell and Victor Wyler
Jerry Yablans
Asher, Morad and Yehuda Zamir
Frederick Zwerling

## $10,000 and Over

Anonymous
Carole and Dr. Allan Abramson
Arthur Adler and Andrea Grossman
Inge and Max Adler
Karen Adler and Larry Greenwald
M. Bernard Aidinoff
Mr. and Mrs. Benjamin Alpert
Mr. and Mrs. Ronald Altman
Jo and Dr. Norman Amer
Daniel and Esther Andron
Mrs. Sarah Aron
Aryeh and Shirley
Karen and Donald Ashkenase
Joel I. Banker
Julian and Sue Barnett
Richard and Eslyn Bassuk
Baumgarten Family
Ellen and Fredric H. Baumgarten
Roberta Caplan Baumgarten and George Baumgarten
Adele and Isidore Becker
Dr. Jerrold M. Becker and Mrs. Rae Becker
Marilyn and Sidney Bender
Mr. and Mrs. Robert Bender and Mr. and Mrs. Andrew Klein
Jack and Giti Bendheim
Arlene and Milton D. Berkman
Mr. and Mrs. Jerome Berko
Judy and Howard Berkowitz
Rochelle and Edward Berkowitz
Jordan and Meredith Berlin
Carol and Jerry Berman
Dr. David H. Berman
Sidney J. Bernstein
Samuel and Iolabee Berson
Ann and Kenneth Bialkin
Dassie and Marvin Bienenfeld
Messrs. Marvin and Julius Bienenfeld, Best Form Fndn.
Ms. Lorilyn Ross Blatt
Enid and Lee Blaymore
Lauren and Jacques Blinbaum
Mr. and Mrs. Peter S. Blumberg
Julia and Norman Bobrow
Mr. and Mrs. Isaac Bodner
Jeffrey and Susan Bogatin
Dr. Alise S. Reicin and Robert P. Boiarsky
Mr. and Mrs. Farhad Bokhour
Rochelle and Moe Bordwin
Barry P. Borodkin
Joan and Mark Boyar
Mr. George Brecher, Esq.
Stanley Brener
Amy and Robert Bressman
Errol H. Brick
Charlotte and Joe Brodie
Joan and Alan Brout
Daniel and Elaine Brownstein
Dr. and Mrs. Eli Bryk
Stewart and Sandra Cahn
Bonnie and Clive Chajet
Norman and Annelyse Chaleff
Michael J. Charles
Ronnie and Laurence Charney
Arthur Chernick
Abe M. and Geri Cohen Foundation
Mr. and Mrs. Alan N. Cohen
Ann and John Cohen
Bryn and Arnold Cohen
Dr. Carmel and Babette Cohen
Eta Gershen and Steven B. Cohen
Lawrence and Lisa Cohen
Mark S. Cohen and Roberta Weinstein Cohen
Dr. and Mrs. Seymour M. Cohen
Stephen and Jeanette Cohen
Dr. and Mrs. M. Donald Coleman
Dr. and Mrs. Morton Coleman
Colin Service Systems Inc.
Rise and Barry Dimson
Rita and Fred Distenfeld
Arlene and Avrom Doft
Mrs. Rosalie Dolmatch
Lorraine and Harold Domnitch
Alison Dreizen
Arthur and Henya Drescher
Ruth Ann Drucker
Tova and Barry Effron
Carole and Gary Eisen
A. Joel Eisenberg and Rose G. Eisenberg Margolis
Mr. and Mrs. David Eisenberg
Eisner & Lubin, Certified Public Accountants
Pamela and Adam Emmerich
Michael N. Emmerman
Harry and Suzanne Engel
Ms. Susan Etra and Mr. Michael Yoeli
Connie and Ray Evans
Mrs. Jane Falk
Mrs. Fred S. Fallek
Mr. Leon Farber
Daniel and Thalia Federbush Foundation
Dr. and Mrs. Donald Feinsod
George and Janet Felleman
Claire and Paul Finkel
Max Finkelstein, Inc.
Stanley P. Fishkin and Nancy S. Marshall
David Fiskus
Edward and Eileen Flax
Robert C. Fleder
Russell and Patricia Fleischman
Dorothy and Donald J. Fleishaker
Hilda and Rudolph Forchheimer
Everett and Robert Fortunoff
Andrew J. Frackman
Andrea and Fred Fraenkel
Susan and Stephen Fraidin
Marla and David Frankel
Michael Frankel
Stanley A. Freed
Robert L. Freedman
Sheila and Robert Friedland
Raphael and Francine Friedlander
Carole and Michael Friedman
Mr. and Mrs. Harry Friedman
Rabbi Herbert A. and Francine Friedman
Isidore and Maralyn Friedman

Louis and Patrice Friedman
Rita and Harry Friedman
Adam Frieman
Mrs. Beatrice Galler
Bruce and Sara Galloway
Bea and Joe Garten
Garwin, Bronzaft, Gerstein and
Fisher
Frank and Sandra Geller
Rabbi Marc Gellman
Helen and Morris Getler
Myrna and Bob Getz
Joel and Eileen Gevarter
Mr. and Mrs. Martin Gevarter
Frances and Jerry Gilberg
Leo and Joan Gilberg
David Gildin
Annora Gilman
Mr. David Glaser and
Ms. Debra Stone
Professor Wladimir Goichman
Mr. Matthew Gold
Mr. Alan Goldberg
Arthur and Carol Goldberg
Lee Goldberg In Memory
of Arthur M. Goldberg
Jeffrey B. Goldenberg
Esther and Jack Goldman
Mr. Robert I. Goldman
Carole and Steve Goldschein
and Family
Adele and Leo Goldschmidt
Susan and David M. Goldsmith
Anita and Stanley Goodman
Ina M. and Arthur S. Gordon
Jackie and Barry Gosin
Mr. James B. Gottlieb
Mr. and Mrs. Laurence S. Grafstein
Morris L. and Charlotte Green
Sholem and Wendy Greenbaum
Alex M. Greenberg, D.D.S.
Meir and Sivia Greenberg
Ms. Gwen M. Greene
Janet and Richard Greenfield
Dr. and Mrs. Allen R. Gribetz
Jane and Efraim Grinberg
Sherman and Sarah Gross
Steven and Georgette Gross
Mr. Walter J. Gross
Robert and Susan Grossman
Helen and Murray Gruber
Peter and Susan Grunthal
Mr. and Mrs. Jeffrey Gural
Elias and Lillian Gurian
Abraham S. Guterman
Lisa and Kenneth Hackel
Ben and Lorelei Hammerman
Dr. Hillel S. Hammerman
Felicia and Nathan Hanfling
Myra and Jonathan Harris
Clare and Jerry Harrison
Gilbert W. and Shelley D. Harrison
Julie and Andrew Hascoe
Deena and Donald Heisler
Lewis and Barbara Henkind
Marilyn and Jerrold Herman
Susan and Stephen Herman
Elliot and Marlene Herskowitz
Morris and Pearl Herson
Mr. and Mrs. Abraham Hiltzik
Marcia and Martin Hirsch
Cindy and Morris Hodkin
and Family
Harold and Ruth Hoffman
Natalie and Joseph Hofheimer
Rabbi and Mrs. Emanuel Holzer
Mr. and Mrs. Mark Honigsfeld
Dr. Albert and
Mrs. Bernice Hornblass
Mr. and Mrs. Joseph Horowitz
Lenore and Michael Hyatt
Fred and Gloria Jacobs
Mr. and Mrs. Gustave Jacobs
Marjorie and Phillip Jacobs
Jerold D. Jacobson
Dr. and Mrs. Julius Jacobson, II
Laurence E. Jacobson
David L. Jaffe
Joan and Jerome Jakubovitz
Mr. and Mrs. Abe Janvey
Jewish Center of Pelham Bay
Cindy S. Johnson
Julian and Barbara Juster
Adam and Estee Kahan
Seth Kaller
George and Louise Kaminow
Rob and Ellen Kapito
Marianne Gold Kaplan and
David Kaplan
Rita J. and Stanley H.
Kaplan Foundation, Inc.
Roslyn and Arthur A. Kaplan
Sylvia and Irving Kaplan
Eileen and Sidney Katz
Helene and Herb Katz
Joyce Gladston and Michael Katz
Seymour and Arlene Katz
Diane Katzin
Julie T. Katzman
Rosalind and Richard Kaufman
Judy and Uri Kaufthal
Mrs. Alan H. Kemper
Howard Kessler, M.D.
Leonard and Robert Kesten
Freida and Bernard Kiefson
Mr. Steven A. Klar
Dr. and Mrs. Maurice Klein
Fran and David Klingsberg
Louis and Rose Klosk Fund
Bobi Klotz
Marin and Irene Kofman
Pat and Nathan Kornfeld
Marcia and Howard C. Kotkin
Betty and Henry Krakeur
Joyce L. Kramer
Lola and Saul Kramer
(Kramer Foundation)
Mrs. Walter Krissel
David A. Kronfeld
Naomi Kronish
Stephen J. Kule
Moshe Labi, MD
Mrs. Jean Landau
Sidney and Ruth Lapidus
Marilyn and Eliot Lauer
Mr. and Mrs. John S. Lawrence
Mr. and Mrs. Alex Lebowitz
Mr. and Mrs. David H. Lee
Eleanor and Carl Leff
Dr. Rona and Dr. Kenneth Legunn
Mark and Diane Lehman
Drs. Martin and Naomi Leib
Dr. and Mrs. Harold Levine
Harvey and Gloria Levine
Bernice M. Levitt
Jack and Marcia Levy -
Arthur and Barbara Levy
Harriet and Herb Lewis
Robert and Ethel Lewis
Gloria and William V. Lewit, MD
Leonard Lichter
Mr. and Mrs. Samuel H. Lindenbaum
Carol and Burton Lipsky
Mark D. Litt
Anna and Norman London
Rabbi Haskel and Audrey Lookstein
Carol and Joseph Low
Lee and Stanley H. Lowell
Rita and Richard Lowenstein
Mr. and Mrs. Albert Lowenthal
Adrienne and Geoffrey Lurie
Rachel R. Brody and
Michael P. Lustig
David and Sondra Mack
Ruth and Bernard L. Madoff
Sion and Sionet Mahfar
Bruce and Elissa Maier
Mr. and Mrs. Henry and
Paula Major
Seymour H. Malamed
Michael Malina
Robert and Fran Malina
Stephanie and Ronald Mann
and Family
Alisa and Barry Mannis
Bonnie and Russell Mannis
Mr. and Mrs. Jeffrey Manocherian
Dr. Hillel Y. Marans
Ms. Shirley Kaplan
Diane and Jeffrey Marks
Ellen R. Marram
Mrs. Dorothy Marx
Hermione Matsil
Jules Mayer
Mr. Alexander Melamid
Joan and Herbert L. Mendelson
Rhena and Harold Mermelstein
Seth and Anne Merrin
Ernest W. and
Amy Goldberg Michel
Dr. and Mrs. Jacob Miller
Sid and Rona Miller
Barbara and Herbert Mines
Ruth and Harry Minkoff
Drs.Julie and Hal Mitnick
Josef and Marsy Mittlemann
Elaine Pohl Moore
Salim and Vahide Morad
Elaine and Ronald A. Morris
Linda and Edward Morse
Alan A. Nadel
Mr. Meyer W. Nathans
Irma and Stanley Neisloss
Linda and Stuart Nelson
Vita and Lester Nelson
Frank Neubauer
Mrs. Hilda R. Neufeld
New Cracow Friendship Society
Carol and Melvin Newman
Drs. Etta and Isaac Novick
Estate of David Nussbaum
Toby and Bernard Nussbaum
Daniel and Jane Och
Mrs. Irma Oestreicher
Dr. and Mrs. Joseph J. Okon
Olan Family
Daniel J. Ordan
Evelyn and Sidney Orenstein
Batsheva Ostrow
Par Plumbing Co., Inc.
Mr. Gordon A. Paris
Viviane and Ira Paris
Dr. and Mrs. Lev Paukman
Irene and Joe Perl
Julius and Jean Perlbinder
Mr. and Mrs. Gerald A. Pinsky
Ira and Carole Pittelman
Jonathan and
Lesley Goldwasser Plutzik
Mr. and Mrs. Lester Pollack
Bonnie and Isaac Pollak
Edward and Lisa Raice
Carol S. Goldstein and
Robert A. Raskin
Sheldon and Joan Ratner
Anne and Harry J.
Reicher Foundation
Mrs. Gila M. Reinstein
Mr. Paul M. Reinstein
Mr. and Mrs. Edward A. Reiss
Elaine Stein Roberts
Jane and H. Richard Roberts
Lisa and Andrew Rodman
Linda and Sidney Rosdeitcher
Mr. and Mrs. Philip Rosen
Stuart and Judith Rosen
Seymour and Anna Rosenberg
Rabbi Jonathan I. and
Tzipporah R. Rosenblatt
Lester and Helen L. Rosenblatt
Sam and Harriette Rosenbloom

Robert Rosenman
Jackie and John Rosenthal
Marjorie Rosenthal
Seymour and Lillian Rosenthal
Merry and Sidney Rosman
Margaret and Carl Ross
Dr. Samuel and Betty Roth
Judith and Harvey E. Rothenberg
Laura and Peter Rothschild
Gerald Alan Rothstein
Miriam and Samuel Rotrosen
Adina and Jeffrey Rubin
Barbara and LeRoy Rubin
Anita and Seymour Rudorfer
Mel and Lea Ruskin
Karen and Stephen Sachs
Paul and Rose Safro
Janet and Marshal Salant
Arnold A. Saltzman
Michael Salzhauer
Grace Sardell
Roslyn Sarezky
Joan and Arthur Sarnoff
Mimi and Howard Sarnoff
Rabbi David Savisky
Mr. and Mrs. Stephen Savitsky
Beverly and Henry Schachar
Mr. and Mrs. Stuart Schapiro
Dr. and Mrs. Sanford C. Scheman
Livia Schenker
George and Ellen Schieren
Myrna and Erwin Schimmel
Susan and Bruce Schlechter
Richard and Betty Schlein
Mr. Ralph Schlosstein
Dr. Moshe and
Rochel Schlusselberg
Stuart and Gail Schneider
Rochelle and Mel Schnell
Ronnie and Andrew Schonzeit
Myra and Milton J. Schubin
Edward and Lenore Schultz
Carmi Schwartz
Carolyn S. Schwartz
Jane and Martin Schwartz
Mark and Lisa Schwartz
Audrey and Fred Schwartzberg
Bonnie and Barry Septimus
Elmer H. Settel
Mr. and Mrs. Stephen Shalom
Mr. and Mrs. Mickey Shamah and
Mr. and Mrs. Steven Shamah
Beatrice and Milton S. Shapiro
Dorothy and Howard Shapiro
Irving M. Shapiro
Dr. Melvin Shay
Judith Adler Sheer
Abner Sheffer
Susan and Nathan Shmalo
Blanche W. and Gerald Shukow
Colette and Willaim D. Siegel
Joyce and Sheldon M. Siegel
Harry and Martha Silber
Mr. and Mrs. Howard Silverman
David and Patty Silvers
Arlene and Bernard Silverstein
Bernard and Ruth Simon
Harriet and Andrew J. Singer
Mr. Peter Siris
Mr. Howard D. Sitzer
David and Rasha Sklar
John H. and Marianne Slade
Donna Auerbach Slotnick
Martin and Judith Sokol
Miriam and Henry Solan
Elsa and Stephen D. Solender
Drs. Audrey Weiner
and Jeffrey Solomon
David and Mary Solomon
Doris and Daniel Solomon
Jeannette Solomon
Zoltan and Dora Sorell
Michael and Lisa Spett
Barry B. Stein, MD
Rabbi Harold and Ruth Stein
Mr. Albert Stern
Joseph and Mildred Stern
Joyce and Henry Stern
Jack and Harriet Stievelman
Mr. and Mrs. Walter Straus
Elaine and Elias Strum
Mr. and Mrs. Stanley H. Sussman
Judith and Irwin Tantleff
Harry and Florence Taubenfeld
Mr. Paul Taubman
Mr. Bertram Teich
Harvey L. Tepner
Cathe and Martin Tepper
George M. and Bernice Thomas
Kenneth and Deborah Tuchman
Diane and Thomas Tuft
Mr. and Mrs. Martin Turchin
Mr. and Mrs. Arnold Turok
Mindy and Marc Utay
Marjorie and Stanley Verby
Mark and Pearl Vogel
Barry and Teri Volpert
Larry and Lilly Wajnberg
Eugene Wallach
Helene & Herb Wallenstein
Peter and Dale Wang
Craig and Marla Wasserman
Mrs. Claire Weidman
Marshall Weinberg
Sara and Ben Weinberger
Mr. and Mrs. Edward A. Weinstein
Peter and Laura Weinstein
Sarah B. Weinstein - Schwartz
Dr. and Mrs. Philip Weintraub
Elaine and Mel Weiser
Barbara and Melvyn I. Weiss
Dr. and Mrs. Daniel Weisz
David and Rebecca Welner
Irving L. Wharton
Ashley and Justin Whitney
Wilson, Elser, Moskowitz,
Edelman and Dicker
Diane and Howard Wohl
Mr. and Mrs. Elliot K. Wolk
Carol Wolowitz
Elaine and Leonard Wurzel
Mr. and Mrs. Robert Yaspan
Leo and Elisabeth Ziegel
Ezra K. Zilkha
Israel and Sylvia Zipes
Dr. Irving and Michele Zoltan
Eugene and Sandra Zwillinger

## $5,000 and Over

Anonymous
Sidney S. and Janeta F. Abelson
Elkan Abramowitz and
Susan Isaacs
Susan Abramowitz and
Aaron Gurwitz
Barry M. Abramson
Herbert and Marion Achtentuch
Ita Josette Ades
Mr. David Adest
Susan and Michael Adin
Mitchell and Maxine Aigen
Ain Family
Mark H. and Cantor Susan B. Alcott
Jo Ann and Paul R. Alter
Rabbi and Mrs. Marc D. Angel
Carol Stone - Applbaum
Leonard and Leonora Arye
Bernice and Jerome W. Ash
May Ashner
Seymour R. Askin, Jr.
Mr. Lawrence Askowitz
Mr. Jozef Atlas
Eileen and Larry Austin
Dr. and Mrs. Ronald J. Avis
Gale and Sheldon Baim
Mr. Jerome E. Ball,
Mr. Lawrence Milowitz and
Mr. Arnold Weinberg, Balson
Hercules Group
Bonnie Barest
Marsha Bassen
Donna and Stanley I. Batkin
Jay M. Bauman, MD
Jack Becker
Joel and Shari Beckman
Ronni and Cy Beer
Mordechai Beizer
Randy and Mark Belnick
Louis H. Benjamin and Lisa Javitch
Alfred and Gayle Berg
Julius and Dorothy Berman
Reuben and Linda Berner
Betsy and Julian Bernstein
Marianne and Harvey Bernstein
Philip and Florence Bernstein
Mr. Yechoua E. Beyda and Family
Mr. Charles Y. Beyda and Family
Mr. Walter Bialo
Matthew S. Blank
Terri Newman and Steven Bleiberg
Paula Blumenfeld and Joe Gantz
M & F Blumenreich Foundation
Renee Bohm
Abba and Sandy Borowich
Sandra Holman Braun
Dr. and Mrs. Michael Braunstein
Simon and Nesi Breines
Stephen A. Brenner
Mr. and Mrs. Paul Brichta
Lester and Miriam Brickman
Mr. and Mrs. Joseph E. Brooks
Kenneth and Noreen Buckfire
Penny Wise Budoff, M.D.
Gidon M. Caine
Hy and Estelle Carroll
Catton Brothers Corporation
Nancy and Joel Hirschtritt and
Alexandra Certilman
Sheila and Don Chaifetz
Stephen Chapin and Deborah Sacks
Ruth Chodos
Evelyn G. Clyman
Henry and Evelyn Cohen
Lawrence Cohen
Marie and Samuel J. Cohen
Mr. Morris E. Cohen
Mr. and Mrs. Stephen P. Colman
Dr. Joel Karmazin Comet
Mrs. Michele Karmazin Comet
Harvey Cooper and Peter Massa
Apex Wire and Cable Corp.
Mr. and Mrs. Harvey Cooper
Paul and Anne Corwin
Marilyn Kanrek Cranney
Toby and Lester Crystal
Mr. and Mrs. Jack Cytryn
Bobbie Sue Daitch
Maxwell and Esther Dane
James and Diana Daniels
Robert E. Decker, M.D.
Rochelle and Henry Dicker
Linda and Bernard Dishy
Pauline and Emanuel Doft
Shirlee and Barry Doft
Elyse and Madeleine Dorkin
Gary K. Duberstein
Messrs. Ebrahim,
Ike and David Eshaghian
Doreen A. and Beryl Y. Eckstein
Cynthia and David Edelson
Mary and Kenneth Edlow
Joan and Martin Eglow
Lois S. and Spencer M. Ehrman
Mr. and Mrs. Saul Eisenberg
Tamar and Alec Ellison
David and Lea Engelman
Mr. and Mrs. Sol Englander
Mr. and Mrs. J. A. Epstein
Mr. Scott Erlich
Mr. and Mrs. Burton J. Esrig
Mrs. Bobbie Falk

George and Ilse Falk
Michael L. Faltischek
The Plum Family
Michael and Roslyn Feder
Phyllis and Bernard Feinberg
Azriel and Toby Feiner
Frayda and Ronald Feldman
Michael J. Feldman
Dr. and Mrs. Sidney S. Feuerstein
Mr. Ralph Fine
Frank I. and Betty Finnel
Iris and John Fisher
Steve and Lelah Fleischer
Dorothy and Donald J. Fleishaker
Jack and Carole Forgash
Foundation-To-Life
Dr. and Mrs. Joshua L. Fox
Frankel & Co., Inc.
The Frederick Loewe Foundation
Hon. and Mrs. Samuel G. Fredman
Marina and Feliks Frenkel
Mr. and Mrs. Eric Freudenstein
Martin S. Fridson
Allan H. Fried
Friedman & Friedman Agency, Inc.
Barbara and Norman Friedman
Helen and Sidney Friedman
Rabbi Hillel and Betsy Friedman
Mark and Marjorie Friedman
Rabbi and Mrs. Morris S. Friedman
Norman E. Friedman
Rosie and Mark Friedman
Dr. and Mrs. Steven I. Friedman
William Frumkin
Michael Fuchs
Susan and Alan Fuirst
Frieda and Roy Furman
Sidney S. Furst
Dr. Walter Gadlin and
Dr. Judith Isaac
Fran and Allen Ganz
Joseph and Charlotte Gardner
Murray Gartner
Helen and
the late Theodore Geffner
Mildred Geiger
Esther and Simon Geldwerth
Arlene and Donald Geller
Solomon and Debra Genuth
Mr. Sander R. Gerber
Mr. and Mrs. Alex E. Gerson
Joan Gerstler
Dr. and Mrs. Zachary Gerut
Alec and Tamar Gindis
Myrna and Myron Ginsberg
Mr. and Mrs. Edward C. Ginsburg
Anita and Stanley Gluck
Mr. and Mrs. George Gluck
Phyllis and Ivan Gluck
Florence and Morris Glucksman
Andrew and Irene Goldberg
Muriel Goldberg
Shepard Goldfein

Mrs. Ephraim Goldfield
Mr. and Mrs. Glenn H. Goldfinger
Phyllis Teicher Goldman
Rose Goldman
Victoria and Lloyd Goldman
Cheryl and Joel Goldschmidt
Mr. and Mrs. Harold D. Goldsmith
Deborah J. Goldstein
Howard M. Goldstein
Mr. and Mrs. Leon Goldstein
Louis and Blanche Goldstein
Aharon and Ruth Golub
Lawrence B. Goodman
Phoebe and Merrill Goodman
Mr. Richard F. Goodman
Abraham Gootnick, M.D.
Joan and Donald J. Gordon
Stephen Gordon and
Deborah Lester
Archie Gottesman and
Gary DeBode
Marilyn and Lawrence Gottlieb
Michael and Avivah Gottlieb
Stuart S. Gould
Mr. and Mrs. Scott H. Goverman
Dr. Martin and Monica Grajower
Bennett and Marcy Grau
Blu and Yitz Greenberg
Dr. Ezra and Edith Greenspan
Richard and Victoria Greif
Judah and Jessica Gribetz
Dr. Solomon I. Griboff
Dr. and Mrs. Elliot A. Grossman
Marilyn H. Grossman
Harriet and Alan Gruber
Max Gruber Associates
Mr. and Mrs. Hy Grubman
Deborah and Marc Guthartz
Blanche Gutstein
Martin Hackel
Mr. Claude S. Hakim
Dr. and Mrs. Yonah Hamlet
Leibel Hannes
Mr. and Mrs. Michael Harounian
David and Jessica Harris
Mr. Jeffrey A. Harris
Maryann and Alvin Harris, M.D.
Mr. and Mrs. Eugene Hartmann
Dr. and Mrs. Marvin L. Hartstein
Thomas and Celine Hecht
Dr. Harold and Eva Hefter
Dr. and Mrs. Keith S. Heller
Richard Hendler
Dr. and Mrs. Walter H. Herbert
Phyllis and Harold Herman
Rabbi and Mrs. Basil Herring
The Jacob Hidary Foundation
Dr. and Mrs. George W. Hindels
Felix and Peri Hirsch
Jerome S. Hirsch
Joan and Charles Hirsch
Philip and Judith Hirsch

Marilyn C. Hofer-Gelmor
Trading Co., Inc.
Pearl and Henry Hofman
Dr. Per H. M. Hollander
Jacob M. Holtzman
Dr. and Mrs. Stuart Horodas
Richard and Linda Horowitz
Sidney and Grace Horowitz
Sidney I. Horwitt
Mr. and Mrs. Robert Howard
Dr. David Hurwitz
Arnold and Wende Hyman
Mr. Richard Dickstein,
Mr. Allen Goldberg,
Dave Goldberg Inc.
Robert and Peggy Insel
Augusta F. and Abraham Irvings
Dr. Howard W. Isenberg
Dr. Zev Isseroff
Irwin and Ann Jacobs
Rabbi Richard Jacobs/
Susan K. Freedman
Steven and Anna Jacobson
Richard and Nancy Jaffee
Jon Jaffess
Mrs. Kathryn R. Jaffin
Jewish Center of Bayside Hills
Tzedakah Campaign, Jewish
Theological Seminary
Dr. and Mrs. Morris Jutcovich
Aaron and Roberta Kaiser
Felecia and Harold Kalb
Morry Kalimian
Paula Kalmanash
Mr. Eric Kaltman
Genesia and Steven Kamen
Robert A. Kandel and
Abby C. Hamlin
Charles and Judith Kandler
and Family
Mr. and Mrs. William Kantrowitz
Mr. and Mrs. Martin H. Kaplan
Naomi Kaplan
James and Nancy Kardon
Mr. and Mrs. Seymour Kary
Karen Spar Kasner and
Jay B. Kasner
Arthur M. Katz
Frances R. Katz
Samuel and Vicki Katz
Mr. Ralph Katzowitz
Greta Kaufman
Mrs. Joan Kaufman
Pearl and Paul Kaufman
Marjorie and Steven Kellner
Sylvia and Kurt Kelman
Lucy and Joel Kerman
Michael and Adina Keschner
Parvin Khoubian
Shelly and Howard Kivell
Mr. Jeffrey Klafter
Fela and Sam Klapholz
Steven A. Klar

Joanne and Haskell Klaristenfeld
Arnold and Frances Klein
Judy Klein
Peter and Nina Klein
Robert and Susan Klein
Michael and Arlene Kleinberg
Shirley Kleinman
Mrs. Susan D. Koch
Ed and Ann Koenig
Esther H. Kolatch
Stuart and Arlene Kolbert
Dr. and Mrs. Jonathan W.
Konovitch
Mark and Esther Kook
Carol and Roy Korins
Mr. Sidney and Rabbi Emily Korzenik
Mrs. Joyce Koslow
Rose H. Kotch
Howard and Marcia Kotkin
Rabbi Doniel Z. Kramer
Milton and Rita Kramer
Irving R. and Rena Mae Krevor
Janet and Jerome Kroll
Rodger and Hillary Krouse
Mr. and Mrs. William M. Kufeld
Mr. and Mrs. Jerome S. Lachs
Mr. and Mrs. Julius Lampert
William and Ronnie Lane
Philip and Rhona Lanzkowsky
Mr. and Mrs. Lee Lasher
Stephen and Naomi Lassar
Mr. and Mrs. Oliver Laster
Mr. and Mrs. Michael Laub
Sanford and Arlene Lavitt
Steve Lawrence
Carolyn Lee
Dr. Harvey and Rochelle Lefkowitz
Anita and Bernie Leibowitz
Agatha I. Leifer
Nathan and Elizabeth Leight
Dr. Gila Leiter and Mr. Jim Lavin
Dr. and Mrs. S. Lerman
Andrew and Leslie Lester
James and Emily Levin
Deanna and Hirschell Levine
Sybil and Arthur Levine
John S. Levy
Jerry Lewart
Marge and Stanley Lewin
Michael M. and Joan S. Lewin
Herbert & Elaine Liebman
Gerta M. Linchitz
Howard and Sharon Lindenauer
Victor and Margaret Linell
Michael Loeb
Jeffrey M. Loewy
Charles Looker
Simon and Esther Lopata
Eugene Lubin
Mr. and Mrs. William M. Lucas
Ludwig Field Altschuler
Family Circle
Gladys C. Luria

Yvonne and David Lurie
Mr. Matthew J. Lustig
Lester Lyons
Russell E. Makowsky and
Melanie A. Katzman
Samuel and Phoebe Makowsky
Joel Mandel
Sam and Vicky Mannis
John and Rosemarie Marciano
Margold, Ersken & Wang
Margolin, Winer & Evans
Mr. Joseph D. Mark
Ms. Meryl L. Schlussel
Edith and Carl Markel
Mr. and Mrs. Herman Markowitz
Diane and Jeffrey Marks
Alan and Joanne Marx
Dr. and Mrs. Robert Matalon
Mr. and Mrs. Robert Matza
Mr. and Mrs. Elliot M. Maza
Beverly and George S. Meissner
Richard and Susan Melchner
Shirley and Shei Meltzer
Robert and Joyce Menschel
Dr. and Mrs. Bernard E. Metrick
Emily Blum and Leon Metzger
Mr. Alfred Miller
Bruce and Cindy Miller
Diane and Stanley Miller
Stanley and Ivy Miller;
Jason and Max
Renee and Jerry Mordfin
Thomas Sachs Morgan
Shaz and Betty Mossanen
Louise and Douglas Mund
Edwin Nadel
Mr. and Mrs. Leonard Naider
Deena J. Nelson
Mr. and Mrs. Howard Nelson
Frank Nestor
Marjorie L. Neu
Peter and Marcy Neumann
Paul and Zelda Neustadt
Joshua Newman
Terri Newman and Steven Bleiberg
Ruth and Jay Norek
Moses and Ester Nussbaum
Abner and Nina Ohebshalom
Mr. and Mrs. Robert Okin
Susan and Steven Orlow
Mitchell Ostrove, CLU
Deanna and William Ostrower
Dr. and Mrs. Lawrence J. Pacernick
Marlene and Marvin Padover
Dr. and Mrs. Winston Paley
The Paris Family
Partners Cleaning Corp.,
Mr. Jeffrey Edelstein
Gary and Corrine Paston
Judith and Robert Paulen
Sharon and Rubin Pikus
Arthur L. Pinchuck
Marilyn and Elliott Platt

Sandra and Morton Porwick
Aaron and Arleen Priest
Dafna and Elliot Prince
Provident Sick and
Benevolent Society, Inc.
Eileen and Milton Putterman
Honey and Michael Rackman
Glenn Reicin
Jonathan and Micki Kaplan Reiss
Mr. Norman Reitman
Renee and Arthur Ritz
Jack L. Rivkin
Albert and Adele Robbins
Mr. Stephen Rogowsky
Allison Rosen
J. Philip Rosen
Sandi and Dan Rosenbaum
Shelly and Werner Rosenbaum
Barbara and Buddy Rosenberg
Eric M. and Helen K. Rosenberg
Judith R. Rosenberg
Louise and Gabriel Rosenfeld
Ruth and Herbert M. Rosenfeld
Blanche Rosenhirsch
Mr. Julius Rosenzweig
Ann and Howard Rosman
Dr. Ira and Elizabeth Roth
Nanci and Larry Roth
Rabbi Sol Roth
David D. Rothbart and
Jane S. Rothbart
Marcia and Philip Rothblum
Mrs. Ann Rothenberg
Rabbi Jacobs and
Deborah Rubenstein
Ms. Nan Foster Rubin
Davis & Gilbert
Howard and Nan Rubin
Edward and Carol Sacks
Patricia and Douglas Sacks
Mr. Henry Salfeld
Arthur and Carol Saltzman
Nina and Julian Sandler
Maryam and Mehrdad Sarraf
Richard Savitt
Seymour and Eve Scharf
Carol and Matthew Scharff
Bernice and Sol Schargel
Marcia and Richard Scheiner
Mrs. Eli Schessel
Mr. and Mrs. Robert J. Schiff
Dr. and Mrs. Emanuel Schiowitz
Linda D. Schloss
Sarita and Larry Schneck
Arthur and Jean Schon
William and Deborah Schrag
Dr. Martin L. and
Susanne Schulman
Bert and Henry Schwartz
Rachel and Stanford Schwartz
Dr. and Mrs. Sidney Schwartz
Diane and Marc G. Schwartzberg
Mr. and Mrs. Herman Schwarz

Marion and Sherwood M. Schwarz
David and Debra Segal
Jerome S. Seiler, M. D.
Sandy and Jerry Seligsohn
Mrs. Edith L. Sennet
Nancy and Stephen Senreich
Renee and Ted Serure
Dr. Jacob Shani
Herbert and Lorraine Shapiro
Mr. and Mrs. Jay B. Shapiro
Selma Shavitz
Mr. and Mrs. Gabriel Shehebar
& Sons
Wendy and Steven Shenfeld
Dr. and Mrs. Arthur Ship
Samuel and Barbara Shrager
Dr. and Mrs. Peter Shrock
Marie Shulsky
Marvin Shulsky
Fay and Bill Shutzer
Shirley and Hy Shwiel
Mrs. Sidney Daiell
Harold and Miriam Siegel
Phyllis M. Siegel
Robert G. Siegel
Shirley Adelson Siegel
Dianne and Stanley Siegelbaum
Ramie and Gerald Silbert
Maida and Howard Silver
William and Renee Silverberg
Mr. and Mrs. Howard A. Silverstein
Abdallah and Francine Simon
Bernard and Ruth Simon
Arlene and Richard Sirlin
Mary Ann and Arthur Siskind
Dr. and Mrs. Steven J. Siskind
Mr. Arnold Skolnick
Rebecca and A. Harry Skydell
James C. Slaughter
Bernard Slavin
Mr. and Mrs. Andrew M. Smith
R. A. Smith
Mr. and Mrs. Robert Thornton Smith
Alisa Sorkin
Irving Aaron - Lorraine Sosnow
Robert and Lisa Spatt
Bernard and Laurie Spear
Sonja and Norton Spiel
Bill and Radine Spier
Star Corrugated Box Company
Barney Softness and Betsy Stark
Marc and Anne-Marie Starr
Flora and Morris Steinberg
Lillian B. Steinberg
Dorothea J. Steindl
Steve and Renée Steinig
James and Beatriz Steinschraber
Mr. and Mrs. Charles W. Stendig
Lawrence M. Stern
Lawrence and Fran Sucharow
Robert G. and Surie Sugarman
Avrohom Yechiel Sukenik
Phyllis and Bernard Sussman

Michael and Bryna Sweedler
William and Adrienne Taft
Bernice S. Tannenbaum
Irwin and Judy Tantleff
Adele and Ronald Tauber
Judy Wesalo Temel and
Charles S. Temel
Rita and Charles L. Tenenbaum
Yehuda and Esther Terner
Dr. and Mrs. Gerald Thurer
Susan H. Tofel
Jacques Torczyner
Gary Trachten
Helene Spielman Torker
Myra and Herman Treitel
David and Ina Tropper
Jean and Raymond Troubh
Mr. and Mrs. Mark Udell
Cheryl and David Unterberg
Dr. and Mrs. Joseph R. Van Dyne
Jill and Harold Verschleiser
Joseph and Meryl Viener
Arthur and Phyllis Wachtel
Miriam and Ira D.
Wallach Foundation
Dr. Leslie Walter and
Paula Walter, Esq.
Mr. Stanley Wasserman
Rabbi and Mrs. Mordecai Waxman
Mr. and Mrs. David S. Weil
Adele L. Weinberg
Hazel I. and Michael J. Weinberger
Marc and Rita Weingarten
Ellen and William Weininger
Ester and Bernard Weinreb
Dr. Alan S. Weinstein
Peni and Mark Weinstein
David and Tina Weisenfeld
Norman I. Weisman
Michael and Tessie Weiss
Dr. Norman Weiss
Allan Weissglass
Polly and Michael Weissman
Roslyn and Walter Weitzner
Dr. and Mrs. Barry Wenglin
Rabbi Marilyn Werman
Sharon and Joseph Wiesel
Don and Elsa Wilen
Mr. Leonard M. Wilson
Greta and Felix Wimpfheimer
Ruth and Kurt Wimpfheimer
The Winkler Foundation
Barry N. and Joan D. Winograd
Dr. Harold A. and
Dorothy B. Wittcoff
Susan Wolff
Helene and Zygfryd Wolloch
Ira Yavarkovsky
Lillian and Aaron Yohalem
Kenneth D. Youner, M.D.
Dr. and Mrs. Melvin Young
Mrs. Leonard Zahn
Helene and Fred Zauder

Michael and Barbara Zimmerman
Lloyd P. Zuckerberg
Mr. Mike Zuckerman,
Mr. Marvin Zuckerman
Dr. Jerome and Gloria Zuflacht
Alan H. Zwiebel

## $1,000 and Over

Anonymous
Andrea and Daniel Aaron
Mary Theresa Abbowdowdola
Sidney S. and Janeta F. Abelson
Elie and Judith Abemayor
Monica and Henry Aboodi
Mr. and Mrs. Harvey Abrahams
Richard K. Abrahams
Harry Abramowitz
Mrs. Lenore Abramowitz
Nira Abramowitz
Mr. and Mrs. Steven M. Abramowitz
Mr. William M. Abrams and Ms. Julie M. Salamon
Mr. Larry Abramsky
Dr. Philip Abramsky
Sandy Acker
Dr. and Mrs. Jacob Ackerman
Mr. and Mrs. Stephen Ackerman
Adco Electrical Corporation
Merv and Thea Adelson
Mr. & Mrs. Alan M. Ades
Arlene and Joseph Adler
Ben and Aviva Adler
Mr. and Mrs. George B. Adler
Gerald Adler
Gunther and Anita Adler
Lillian and Arthur Adler
Mr. and Mrs. Sidney G. Adler
Mr. Mitchel and Mrs. Ellen Agoos
Edith H. Agus
Irving J. Aibel Foundation, Inc.
Harvey W. Aiges, M.D.
Dorothy Ain
Alex and Ita Aingorn
Leo and Edith Aisenman
Harold and January Akselrad
Gerald Aksen
Iris Alex
Jack Alexander
Harriet and Mel Alifanz
Mr. and Mrs. Andrew Alisberg
Mark and June Alpert
Robert Altabet
Beth and Stuart Alter
Susan and Ira Altfeder
Naomi C. Altschul
Stanford M. Altschul
David and Linda Altshuler
Philip and Martha Amarant
Jeffrey Amer and Audrey Peltz
Raphael Amoona
Salvador Amram
Rabbi Ronald and Nancy Androphy
Rhoda and Leonard Anker
Alan I. Annex
Sanford L. Antignas
Alfred Appel
Dr. Susan Bernstein Aranoff
Anne and David Arbeit
Harvey and Barbara Arfa
Mr. and Mrs. Isaak Aronin
Mr. and Mrs. Raymond L. Aronson
Richard S. Aronson
Daniel Lewis Aronstein
Ellen Aschendorf Shasha
Jack Aschendorf
Lawrence I. Atlas
Elliot and Rita Auerbach
Judy Auerbach
Joy and Avi Avidan
Barbara and Frank Axel
Dr. and Mrs. George Axelrad
E J B
Jessica Bacal, Esq.
Philip L. Baer
Dr. and Mrs. Saul Bahn
Dr. and Mrs. Henry H. Bahr
Gerald Baker
Suzanne and Kenneth Bakst
Renée Ball
Robert J. Ball
Blossom and Jack Balsam
Moses Balsam
Mr. Eli J. Band
Banking, Finance and Wall Street/ Unit #5252 B'nai B'rith
Louise Chazen Banon
Dr. and Mrs. Jacob S. Barb
Howard Barbanel
Dr. Laura Barbanel
Mrs. Lilyan Barchoff
Mr. Ronald S. Baruch
Mr. and Mrs. Harold R. Bassen
Amy Batkin
Mr. and Mrs. Morton Batlan
Lore Bauer
Rosele Bauer
John E. Baumgardner, Jr.
Ellen R. Bayer
Joseph Beck
Dr. and Mrs. Joel Becker
Shari and Joel Beckman
Constance Begelfer-Lambert
Steven Begleiter and Karen Saponar
Shirley and Sol Behmoiram
Judith and Matthew Beizer
Michelle Friedman and Benjamin Belfer
Bob and Brandi Bell
David J. Bell
Claire and Bernard Beller
The Benaid Foundation
Lonny Benamy and Maidelle Goodman Benamy
Susan and Jack Bender
Shirley G. Benerofe
Karen L. Bennett
Georgette Bennett-Tanenbaum
Scott and Cheryl Benson
Kivette and Barry Benton
Miriam and Conrad Berenson
Edith Berg
Dr. Richard and Judy Berg
Gilda and Melvin H. Berger
Jane Berger
Max and Dale Berger
Pearl and David Berger
Howard and Corinne Berke
Mr. and Mrs. Alfred Berkovits
Mr. and Mrs. Barry Berkowitz
Mr. Bernard W. Berkowitz
Michael and Lisa Berkowitz
Hon. Michael Stallman and Ms. Jacqueline Berkowitz
Nathan and Sondra Berkowitz
Daniel B. and Gisela H. Berkson
Matthew K. Berler
Roy and Bess Berlin
Mr. and Mrs. Andrew S. Berman
Dr. and Mrs. Daniel S. Berman
Mr. and Mrs. Len Berman
Ronni and Kenny Berman
William Berman
William and Patricia Berman
Alison and Edward Bermant
Harold Bernanke
Alan S. Bernikow
Irving and Judith Bernstein
Joseph and Carmela Bernstein
Lewis and Donna Bernstein
Drs. Lewis and Gaya (Aranoff) Bernstein
Marianne and Harvey Bernstein
Philip and Anne Bernstein
Stacee and Jeffrey Bernstein
Vera and Aaron Bernstein
Vivian Bernstein
David L. Berstein
Roslyn W. Besdine
Dr. and Mrs. Allan Beyda
Mr. and Mrs. Morris E. Biederman
Barbara and Jack Bigio
Muriel and Nathan Bilger
Deborah Hilsenraln Bindler and Paul Bindler
Irma Birnbaum
Evelyn and Isaac Blachor
Erna Blade
Mr. and Mrs. Leonard Blaifeder
Ms. Barbara Blank
Dr. and Mrs. Zvi Blaustein
Wilma Sophie Blecher
Madeline and Alan Blinder
Roni and Yehuda Blinder
Lester and Ilene Bliwise
Dr. and Mrs. Sana Bloch
Mrs. Hedy E. Block
Henry Bloom
Annette Blum
Nina Krauthamer and Charles F. Blum
Mr. and Mrs. Robert A. Blum
Mr. and Mrs. Peter S. Blumberg
David and Karen Blumenthal
Mr. and Mrs. Isidor Blumenthal
Dr. Norman Blumenthal
Ellen and William A. Blumstein
Dr. and Mrs. Mordecai Bluth
Dr. and Mrs. Franklin Bocian
Mrs. Irene Bogoff
Robert S. Bookman
Albin H. Boome
Mr. and Mrs. Barry Boonshaft
Steven and Susan Boughner
David and Evelyn Bousel
Mr. and Mrs. Daniel Boyarsky
Dr. and Mrs. Michael J. Bradford
Jeffrey Branman
Ruth Braslow
Sora and Shlomo Brazil
Mildred Supnick Brecker
Murray R. Breidbart
Corey and Rose Breier
Simon and Nesi Breines
Henry and Anne Brenner
Martin I. and Shirley B. Bresler
Alan and Shirley Bresnick
Edward A. Brill and Miriam L. Siroky
Elaine and Howard Broder
Hannah N. Broder
Thomas L. Brodie
Mr. Bert E. Brodsky
Doris Brody
Sheila Brody
Dr. and Mrs. Harold Bronheim
Rabbi Lester Bronstein and Cantor Benjie Ellen Schiller
Natalie Finkelstein Bronster
Felice and Gary Brooks
Mr. and Mrs. Mitchell J. Brooks
Robert and Devorah Brooks
Alvin H. Broome
Betty Schneider Brown
Robert B. Brown
Shirley and Joe Brown
Sylvia K. Brownstone
George T. Bruckman
Dr. and Mrs. Keith Brumberger
David and Harriet Bryk
Estie and Joel Bryk
Dr. and Mrs. Lawrence Bryskin
The Buchwald Family - Nat, Rhoda, Benjamin and Hyman
Phyllis and Bruce Buckler
Rabbi Howard and Laura Buechler
Kathryn and Martin Bunin
Norman A. Cagin
Mrs. Lee Calicchio
Jonathan H. Canter
Raphael and Lonnie Capon

Lois and Alan Carus
Peter J. Caust
Elinor Ceresney
Joy Brownstein and David Chalfin
Mr. and Mrs. Sy Charney
Stanley and Doris Charnoff
Morris and Penny Charytan and Family
Barbara Chasen, Ph.D, President, Introductions Club
Mr. and Mrs. Irving J. Chaykin
Kathy A. Chazen, CLU, CHFC
Dr. Oscar and Marilyn Check
Ben and Betty Checkanow
Charles M. and Sharon L. Chernick
Daniel and Vivian Chill
Halina Chryzman, Nee Karafiol
Alvin L. Chumsky
Howard and Barbara Cinamon
Arthur and Frances Citrin
Pauline and Roy Clements
Anni, Michael and Gloria Coden
Albert I. and Lenora Coe
Mr. and Mrs. Harris N. Cogan
Roslyn and Harold Cohan
Abby Joseph Cohen and David Cohen
Annette A. Cohen, M.D. and John M. Feder, M.D.
Ms. Arline Bystock Cohen
Carol and Edward Cohen
Dov and Susan Cohen
Evan J. Cohen
Mr. and Mrs. Gary I. Cohen
Harold and Suri G. Cohen
Drs. Harris and Sandra Cohen
Hindy and Seymour Cohen
Mr. Jerry Cohen
Joanne Drexler Cohen
Hon. Joseph Cohen
Dr. Karen Kostroff and Dr. Jon Cohen
Mr. and Mrs. Marty Cohen
Dr. and Mrs. Michael Cohen
Milton and Lita Cohen
Naomi and Charles Cohen
Philip and Danielle Cohen
Suzanne M. Cohen
William W. and Eva Cohen
Donald and Eva Cohn
Myron Cohn
Y. B. Cohn
Robert Coleman
Bobbi and Barry Coller
Theodore and Shoshana Comet
Congregation Beth-El of Massapequa, N.Y.
Alice and Richard Conrad
Shirley Conrad
Marcia Cooper
Robert and Joan Cooperman
Mimi Copeland
Renee and Dr. Stuart Copperman
Rabbi and Mrs. Joel Corn
Judith and Erwin Corwin
Betty Cotton
Edward and Lesley Cowen
Cradle Tots, Inc., Irving Maleh, Murray Maleh and Joe N. Shalom
Dr. and Mrs. Stanley H. Craig
Dr. and Mrs. Edward Crane
Dr. and Mrs. Alan Crystal
Rabbi Darryl P. Crystal
Mr. and Mrs. Eugene Cummings
Carole and David Curtis
Ms. Rose Cusumano
Robert and Marilyn Damast
Alex and Monica Dannenberg
Seymour Dashow
Dr. Sami S. David
Suzanne J. Davidson
Daniel N. Davis
Jean Davis
Mr. Laurence E. Capuano and Mr. Jack Debehar
Mr. and Mrs. Lester E. Degenstein
Dr. Barnet Delson
Sheldon H. Deluty, M.D.
Dr. Warren and Sheryl Deluty
Dr. and Mrs. Lewis H. Dennis
Jetty Dentz
Mr. and Mrs. Sol Dentz
Ronnie and Myles Desner and Family
Laraine and Hy Diamond
Michael and Deena Diamond
Dr. William Diamond
Dr. Ronald Kahn
Dr. Laurie Kasnicki
Dr. and Mrs. David J. Dickoff
Denise Dimson
Rochelle Stein Dincesen
Laurie S. Disick
Dean I. Dobbin, M.D.
Jechil and Sally M. Dobekirer
Mr. Jacob Doft
Daniel L. Dolgin and Loraine F. Gardner
Morris and Delores Dolnane
Eric and Mariel Donath
Eric and Marleen Donnenfeld
Stephen Doochin and Cheryl Sandler
Mr. Arthur J. Draznin
Mr. and Mrs. Dennis J. Drebsky
Sylvia A. Dresner
Andrew J. Drexler, M.D.
Richard Dubin, M.D.
Capt. Morris G. Duchin, USN, Ret.
Walter and Lillian Dulken
Mr. and Mrs. Irwin Dunn
Mrs. Mildred Dworetz
Raquel and David Dykaar
Hon. Lawrence and Lynne Ecker
Mr. and Mrs. Steven G. Eckhaus
Felice and Arthur Eckman
Laurence E. Eckstein
David and Marsha Edell
Dr. David S. Edelstein
Dr. Martin and Esther Ehrenberg
H. Steven Ehrenhalt
Freda and Judge M. Arthur Eiberson
Joseph and Vicki Eichenbaum
Gloria and David Eiseman
Judith and Alan Eisenman and Family
Terry and Dennis M. Eisenberg
Carole and Richard Eisner
Karen Lehmann-Eisner and David F. Eisner
Sylvia Elan
Myrna and Sheldon Elfenbein
Jay Eliezer
Dr. and Mrs. Gilad Ellenberg
Dorothy Elowitch
Joann and Mark Engel
David and Lea Engelman
Binah and Danny Englander
Jennifer Englander
Nancy Fisher Englander
Dr. and Mrs. Sasha Englard
Bonnie Englebardt
Barbara Epstein
Rabbi Gilbert M. Epstein
Helen and Edward M. Epstein
George Eichmann and Marianne E. Erdos
Sarah K. Erlij
Hy "Bunny" Escava
Linda and Allen Essner
Polly Etkind
Lior and Susan Evan
Hal and Maria Evans
Drs. Richard and Nina Evans
David and Judith Ezekiel
Peter R. Ezersky
Dr.and Mrs. Edward Ezrick
John Fabiani
Marcy Sonneborn Fabiani
Sara Fabrikant
Mrs. Adeline Failkow
Lawrence Failkow
Gerda Falbel
Oscar N. Falk
Mr. Louis Falkenstein
Sema and Martin Farbstein
Steven Fasman, Esq.
Mr. Michael S. Fassler
Faith and Harry Feder
Frances Shreiber Feder
Meir Feder
Miriam Feder
Dr. and Mrs. Morris J. Feder
Dr. and Mrs. Walter Feder
Elsa and Melvin Federbush
Dr. Avi and Mrs. Federgrun
Raymond Feiden
Henry M. and Miriam Feiereisen
Dr. and Mrs. Eugene B. Feigelson
Karen Misler and Barry S. Feigenbaum
Mr. Andrew K. Feigenberg
Mr. and Mrs. David Feinberg
Mae K. Feinberg
Nathan Feinman
Joan Lucks Feinstein
Ms. Joan Lucks Feinstein
Martin Feinstein
Dr. Neil Feinstein
Linda Gail Feinstone
Jessica and David Feldan
Jay N. and Nancy Feldman
Mindy and Andrew Feldman
Robin and Stuart Feldman
Sharon and Jeff Feldman
Jonathan and Lori Feldstein
Bernice and Marvin Feller
Marcia Feltheimer
Laurie Cohen Fenster
Rabbi and Mrs. Myron M. Fenster
Mr. Yale M. Fergang
Eugene Fernbach
Maury L. Fertig
Sarah Fertig
Marilyn Feuer
Mr. and Mrs. Corey R. Shanus, Mr. and Mrs. Phillip Feuer
Rona B. Feuer
Dr. Ignace Feuerlicht
Dvora Fields
Harry and Barbara Fields
Ida and Raymond Fields
Michael and Linda Fields
Bunny and Bernie Filler
Mrs. Fannie L. Fine
Lillian and Morton Fine
The Finerman Foundation Inc.
Dolly and Barry Fink
Dr. and Mrs. Noah S. Finkel
Adele and Bernard Finkelstein
David Martin Finkelstein
Dr. and Mrs. Harvey Finkelstein
Dr. Joseph Finkelstein
Marsha and Lou Finkelstein, Matt, Will and Julia
Patricia Finkelstein
Phyllis and Harvey Finkelstein
Laurie Cohen Finster
Ralph W. Firman
Shoshana Raviv Firman
Lorraine and Albert Firstman
Lionel and Ruth Fisch
Myra and Joe Fisch
Bob and Shelley Fischel
Mr. and Mrs. Douglas C. Fischer
Martin A. Fischer
Mr. and Mrs. Robert W. Fischer
Linda and Roger Fisher
Martin and Miriam Fisher
Phylis S. Fisher
Robert M. Fisher
Carole and Cliff Fishman

David Fishman and Mindell Seidlin
George and Eudys Fishman
Herman and Eunice Fishman
Ingrid Fishman
Ira Z. Fishman
Lynne and Joshua Fishman
Robert J. Fishman
Vicki and Joseph Fishof
Mr. and Mrs. Lester G. Fixell
Martin J. Flashner
Constance and Mitchel Flaum
Rose L. Flax
Jane S. Flechner and
Ronald Schechter
Alan and Martha Fleischer
Mr. and Mrs. Elliot Fleischer
Robert S. Fleischer and
Susan L. Raanan
Shirley S. and William R. Fleischer
Grace S. and Howard S. Fleischman
Mona and Jerry Fleisig
Arthur and Janet Fliegelman
Jerry Flint
Elaine and James Flud
Barbara and Edward Fogel
Rabbi Daniel and Eleanor Fogel
Diane and Blaine Fogg
Maxine M. Foreman
Blanche Forman
Dr. and Mrs. Donald Forman
Linda and Daniel Forman
Brauna and Marvin Fortgang
Dr. Grover V. Foster Jr.
Mr. Leonard Fox
Cecele and Francis Fraenkel
Nancy and Rob Fraiman
Harriet Frank
Hilda Frank
Mimi and Alan Frank
Syril and Walter A. Frank
Virginia and Larry Frank
Arthur Frankel
Evelyn and Arthur Frankel
Vera B. Frankel
Ruth and Daniel Frankfurt
Rabbi Stephen and Karen Franklin
Mrs. Helen Freedman
Dr. & Mrs. Michael L. Freedman
Dr. Gerald Freilich
Nicholas Freund
Adele and Dan Fried
Arthur K. Fried
Maurice Fried
Stanley Fried
Esther and Arthur Friedberg
Rae Nadler Friedenberg
Fred Friedfeld
Dr. Beatrice L. Friedland
Rita Friedland
Dr. Emanuel A. Friedman
Ms. Harriet Friedman
Henrietta and Sol Friedman
Dr. and Mrs. Ira H. Friedman
Mr. Irving Friedman
Joel M. Friedman, D.D.S.
Gary and Kristin Friedman
Dr. and Mrs. Kenneth Friedman
Laurette Friedman
Lewis Friedman
Melinda and David Friedman
Nancy and Robert Friedman
Mr. Phillip Friedman
Ruth L. Friedman
Susan O. Friedman
Valerie Jo Friedman
William Friedman and
Annette Jaffe
Marian and Henry Froehlich
Arlene and Richard Fromewick
Ida Fryd
Patti and Wayne Fuchs
Lila Fudalowitz
Elaine Grinthal Fuhrman
Elaine and James Fuld
Bernice and Bernard Futter
Dr. and Mrs. Saul C. Futterman
Alex and Patricia Gabay
Shirley and Ken Gabel
Irma and Robert Gal
Galaxy Freight Service LTD
Marian and Samuel Galewitz
Dr. and Mrs. Lawrence J. Galinkin
Rosalind and Daniel Galinson
Laly and George Gallantz
Ronald A. Garfunkel
Bernard and Ethel Garil
Howard and Phyllis Garlick
Murray M. and Rosalie L. Garren
Mr. and Mrs. Jay C. Garten
Anne and Seymour Gartenberg
Joshua and Carol Gat
Dr. Hal Geliebter
Mr. and Mrs. Jan Geliebter
Arline and Donald Geller
Martin Geller
Pearl and Stanley A. Geller
Edward Gellman
Joey and Ricki Genachowski
Mr. and Mrs. Marc A. Gerber
Ezra and Ethel Gerberg
Eda and Leonard Geringer
Mr. and Mrs. Harold I. Geringer
Mrs. Saul Gersen
Lynne and Richard Gershman
Mr. Alan Jay Gerson
The Ruth and Louis Gerstle
Foundation, Inc.
David and Janet Gerstman
Dr. Israel Getman
Allan Gettleman
Dorothy Gilbert
Marilyn and Harvard Gilbert
Elaine S. Gilde
Faye and Jack Gingold
Adele and Benedict Ginsberg
Linda A. Ginsberg and
Clifford A. Hudis
Myrna and Myron Ginsberg
Mrs. Joan Ginsburg
Rabbi Bruce and Rachel Ginsburg
Bernice and Milton Gitenstein
Dr. and Mrs. Arthur H. Gladstein
Lenore Z. Gladstone, M.D.
Shirley and Saul Gladstone
Donald and Ricky Glasel
Dr. and Mrs. Morton L. Glaser
Barbara and Bruce Glasser
David Glasser
Debby Glasser
Sara and Robert Glasser
Marion Glasserow and
Norman Gladney Glasserow
Herman and Amy Glaswand
The Michael Glatt Family
JoAnne Glazer
Linda Glazer
Harvey and Yetta Glick
Mrs. Mildred L. Glimcher
Mr. Lawrence A. Glinzman
Nancy and David Gluck, M.D.
Renée Kamm Goff
David and Bassie Gold
John and Rose Gold
Mr. Abraham J. and Leah Goldberg
Burton and Rita Goldberg
Edward and Susan Goldberg
Mr. Eugene Goldberg
Mrs. Gertrude Goldberg
Mr. Harold H. Goldberg
Joshua Rabb Goldberg
Leo and Rochelle Goldberg
Matilda G. Goldberg, President,
Sisterhood of
Park Avenue Synagogue
Mrs. Mildred Goldberg
Raymond M. and
Elana Daniels Goldberg
Mr. Robert Goldberg
Roz Goldberg
Samuel Goldberg
and Sons Foundation
Michael P. and Sharon Golden
Dr. and Mrs. Ronald A. Golden
Hortense Goldenberg
Mrs. Dorothy Goldfinger
Mr. and Mrs. Shelby Goldgrab
Hope M. Golding
Amy and Cliff Goldman
Mr. Barry Goldman
Harvey P. Goldman and
Sabra B. Goldman
Peter J. Goldman
Fred and Ruth Goldschmidt
Ruth Goldschmidt
Gerald P. and Leda C. Goldsmith
Paul J. Goldsmith
Penny Goldsmith
Dr. and Mrs. Stanley J. Goldsmith
Arthur and Caryl Goldstein
Blanche and Louis Goldstein
Garson K. and
Susan M. S. Goldstein
Jack and Edna Goldstein
Leila and Bert Goldstein
Michael and Roberta Goldstein
Milton and Miriam Goldstein
Rena and Mark Goldstein
Stephen and Mona Goldstein
Syd Rossman Goldstein
Tara and Wayne Goldstein
Terry and Ira J. Goldstein
Mr. Wayne K. Goldstein,
Ms. Tara Goldstein
James and Carol Goldwater
Larry and Sandi Goller
Evelyn and Alfred Gollomp
Judy and Azriel Golowa and Family
Jose E. Gonzales
Mr. and Mrs. Jonathan B. Goodblatt
Barbara and Herbert Goodfriend
David Goodman
Jay S. Goodman
Zmira and Anthony Goodman
Jack and Paula Gora
Alan M. Gordon
Barbara and Maxwell Gordon
Cheryl and Arthur I. Gordon
Mr. David M. Gordon
Mark Forrest Gordon
Maxwell Gordon
Rabbi Dr. Morton L. Gordon
Ruth and I. Lewis Gordon
Sharon and Eric Gordon
Mr. and Mrs. Sheldon Gordon
Sylvia P. Gordon
Rabbi Morris S. Gorelik
Phyllis and Paul Gorfinkel
Drs. Jack and Lauren Gorman
Bilha and Jerry Gottlieb
Dr. and Mrs. Fred Gottlieb
Mr. Richard W. Gottlieb
Mrs. Marcia Gould
Mrs. Lorraine Grabel
The Grauman Family
Ruth and David Gravitz
Leslie and Richard Grazi
Allen Green
Andrew J. Green and
Patricia L. Speier
Richard S. Green
Gail and Steve Greenbaum
Scott Greenbaum, M.D.
Dr. and Mrs. Abraham S. Greenberg
Doree and Chuck Greenberg
Linda and Saul Greenberg
Mr. Matt A. Greenberg and
Ms. Debra R. Greenberg
Dr. and Mrs. Saul N. Greenberg
Dr. and Mrs. Stanley Greenberg
Mr. and Mrs. Bruce Greenfield
Mrs. Eva Miller Greenfield

Lena and Martin Greenfield
Greenspan Associates Inc.
Rabbi and Mrs. Joseph Greenstein
David D. Greenwald
Steven and Alice Greenwald
Carol and Ira Greifer
Louise and James Greilsheimer
Stanley and Rita Grey
Irwin and Harriet Gribetz
Drs. Martin and Amy Fox Griffel
Irene Schiff Groban
Estelle and Maury Gromet
Rabbi Abraham Gross, Cong. Shaare Hatikvah Inc.
Mr. and Mrs. Bertold Gross
Mrs. Frances K. Gross
Leonard J. Gross
Dr. and Mrs. Ludwig Gross
Louis and Ceil Grossman
Marc and Leslie Grossman
Mark and Martha Grossman
Ralph Grossman
Rabbi Susan Grossman
Emily Grotta
Sheba and Jack Gruber
Rabbi Zvi Grumet
Larry and Sharon Grunfeld
Dr. Paul and Dr. Katherina Kroo Grunfeld
Shelley Grunfeld
Peter and Susan Grunthal
Dr. Jeffrey L. Gurian
Elise and Robert Gurmankin
Bruce and Amy Gutenplan
Herb and Sylvia Gutenplan
Addie J. Guttag
David Guttman, M.D.
Mr. and Mrs. Harvey Guzik
Mrs. Rickie Halperin Haas
Jill Jacobs and Frederic Haber
Avital Louria Hahn
Raphy and Richard Haimowitz
Dvora and Ephraim Haimson
Beth and Ari Hait
Robert and Stephanie Halio
Nettie and Sidney Halitzer
Dr. and Mr. Stephen R. Hall
Lucy and Richard Halperin
Mr. and Mrs. Allen Halpern
Bernard Halpern
Ivan and Marilyn Hametz
Mrs. Caren Hammerman
Paul and Suzanne Hanau
Lawrence and Sara Handelsman
Milton Handler
Chaya and Sherri Harari
Fran and Carl Harnick
Mr. and Mrs. Robert Harow
Bella and Jacob Harris
Mr. Neil Harrow
Rita and Murray Hartstein
Eric and Patricia Harvitt
Shelly and Neil Harwayne
Jules J. and Arlene Haskel
Leah and Ira Hauser
Mitchell Haviv
William H. Hayden
Howard L. Haykin
Joel L. Hecker
Loraine T. Hecker
Audrey B. Heckler
Mr. Arthur Heiman
Ralph and Michele Heiman
Ruby and Frederick Heiman
Mrs. Judith Heisler
Arleen and Dr. Douglas Held
Susan and Jonathan Held
Dr. Howard Heller
Laurie and Gary Heller
Mildred and Alvin K. Hellerstein
Egon and Mina Henner
Judith and Lester Henner
Dr. Avraham Henoch
Scott and Lisa Henry
Michael and Nancy Herman
Ron and June Hersh
Mark A. Hershey
Richard and Donna Hershman
Rabbi and Mrs. William Herskowitz
Rachel and Benjamin Hersonsky
Roger J. Herz
Bruna and Siegfried Herzfeld
Karen and Ronald Herzog and Children
Walter W. and Barbara F. Hess
Marvin and Laurie Heyman
Andrew and Jody Heyward
Max Hilfstein
Mr. Leemar A. Hill
Howard Hiller
Mr. and Mrs. Stuart V. Himmelfarb
Robert and Eloise Hintersteiner
Ms. Dorothy Dorene Hirsch
Dr. Norman and Louise Hirsch
Reva and Glenn Hirsch
Richard, Christine, David, Catherine and Sarah Hirschman
Adele Hochbaum
Allen and Sue Hochberg
Rabbi Shlomo and Karen Hochberg
Barbara and Simcha Hochman
Richard and Carol Hochman
Judy and Henry Hoenig
Lillian and Jerry Hoenig
Mr. Howard Hoffen
Dr. and Mrs. Alexander Hoffer
Bunny and Jack Hoffinger
Mr. and Mrs. Israel Hoffman
Jonathan and Marjorie Hoffman
Rabbi Lawrence A. and Sally Hoffman
Ronald and Alice Hoffman
Steven and Fran Hoffman
Dr. William Hoffman
Pearl and Henry Hofman
Arthur H. Holtz
Jonathan and Eveline Honig
Dr. and Mrs. Howard Honigman
Lionel Hope, deceased June 1994
Drs. Isaac Weisfuse and Evelyn Horn
Shirley and Leonard Horn
Bob Horne and Laurie Lindenbaum
Mrs. Frances K. Horowitz
Helen K. and Jacob L. Horowitz
Mr. Irwin Horowitz
Mr. and Mrs. Morris Horowitz
Stanley and Elaine Horowitz
William Houslanger
Mrs. Enid S. Howard
Kurt and Jeanette Hurst
Steven A. Hurwitz
Thelma Hurwitz
Helen and Avrum Hyman
Mr. and Mrs. Henry Hyman
Lawrence and Cara Nash Iason
David W. Ichel
Eleanor and Aaron Ignal
Fredric and Marcie Imberman
Sylvia and Irving Inkeles
Irene and Leo Irvings
Mrs. Frances Irwin
Jeffrey Isaacs
Shari and David A. Isacowitz
Jaclyn and Sol Israel
Mr. and Mrs. Sidney Itzkowitz
In Memory of Dorothy Jabin
Rabbi Ian and Suri Jacknis
Lorian Jacks
Nancy K. Jacobowitz
Dalia and Donn Jacobs and Family
Henry and Gloria Jacobs
Julia Jacobs
Miriam Jacobs
Dr. and Mrs. Stephen Jacobs
Arnold N. Bressler and Monica R. Jacobson
Cynthia J. Jacobson
Marshall and Beverly Jacobson
Nanci and Robert Jacobson
Henry and Doris Jacoby
Sandy and Richard Jacoby
Mr. and Mrs. Steven F. Jacoby
Bernard Jaffe Jr.
Dr. George and Matty Jager
Martha Jakes
Rae and Richard Janvey
Isaac and Shoshana Jaroslawicz
Louis H. Benjamin and Lisa E. Javitch
Rona Javitch
Bob and Barbara Jayson
Aryeh and Sura Jeselsohn
Mr. Alexander Jodidio
Samuel and Susan Joffe
Ms. Harriet Josefowicz
Michael E. Joseph
Stanford and Harriet Joseph
Lisa and Michael Josephson
Dr. Daniel Justman
Dr. and Mrs. Edward Jutkowitz
Leo and Claire Kadet
Erna Kahan
Sidney Kahan
Arthur and Eleanor Kahn
Mrs. Eva Kahn
Hodie Kahn
Dr. Max A. Kahn
Michael H. and Phyllis Kahn
Miriam and Eli Kahn
Mrs. Natalie Kahn
Mrs. Shirley D. Kalb
Ira N. Kalfus, M.D.
Judith and Irwin Kallman
Mr. and Mrs. David Kallus and Family
Dr. and Mrs. Jed C. Kaminetsky
Eva and Leonard Kaminsky
Mr. Robert E. Kandel
Mr. and Mrs. Max Kandler
Daniel and Susan Kane
Michael and Judith Kane
Paul M. Kane
Victor and Beatrice Kane
Phyllis and Michael Kann
Dr. and Mrs. Mitchell Kaphan
Drs. Barry and Rosalind Kaplan
Joseph S. and Lily C. Kaplan
Joseph and Miriam Kaplan
Dr. Lawrence and Janet S. Kaplan
Mrs. Lilly Kaplan
Judge and Mrs. Louis I. Kaplan
Margarite and Jim Kaplan
Marshall G. Kaplan
Miriam and Joseph Kaplan
Mr. and Mrs. Robert Kaplan
Sylvia and Oscar Kapnick
Mr. and Mrs. William W. Karatz
Ms. Mona M. Karff
Mrs. Beatrice Karp
Jeffrey Randall Karp
Selma and Norman Karr
Lee Karsch
Dr. Harold M. and Sara Lee Kase
Francine S. Stein and Samuel S. Kasoff
Barbara and Bentley Kassal
Zeena and Harry Kassel
Mr. and Mrs. David Kaszovitz
Edith and Seymour Katcoff
Carol and Richard Kates
Beth Ann Katleman
Ascher and Barbara Katz
Caroline Katz
Ms. Ethelyn Katz
Harvey L. and Glory W. Katz
Dr. and Mrs. Jack Katz
Mr. and Mrs. Leslie Katz
Mr. Robert Katz
Rose and Isidore Katz
Drs. Barbara and Harvey Katzeff
Bruce M. Kauderer

Ann F. Kaufman
Barbara and Jon M. Kaufman
Beth L. Kaufman
Mr. and Mrs. Carl J. Kaufman
Karen and David Kaufman
Lilli Kaufman
Rachel Kaufman
Ruth J. Kaufman
Uri Kaufman
Roberta and Rick Kay
Paul Kaye
Rose Kaye
Alex Jay Keller, M.D.
Isidore Keller
Mr. and Mrs. William Kellman
Dr. Harold Keltz
Mrs. Lida Keltz
Dr. and Mrs. Donald S. Kent
Dr. and Mrs. Ben Kershenbaum
Dr. and Mrs. Joel Keschner
Rony and Ellen Kessler
Roselyn and Howard Kessler
Stuart and Isabel Kessler
Martin and Ruth Kest
Dr. Paul Dince and
Dr. Clarice Kestenbaum
Judith K. Kieval
Mrs. Inez L. Kimmel
Mr. and Mrs. Morton Kimmel
Garrie Kirschbaum
Myron and Esther Kirschbaum
Dr. and Mrs. Marc Kirschner
Ruth and Kenneth Kirschner
Adele Kitchner
Drs. Daniel Javitt and Reba Kizner
Elissa Kraut Klapper
Sandy and Ed Klar and Family
Rabbi Michael and
Rahel Musleah Klayman
Murray and Adele Kleiman
Drs. Andrew and Alma Klein
Dr. and Mrs. Arthur Luce Klein
Mr. and Mrs. Dennis R. Klein
and Family
Elenor Klein
Mr. and Mrs. George Klein
Michael H. Klein
Dr. Michael Klein
Rabbi Stephen and Joanne Klein
Sarah Klein
Mr. Steven Howard Klein
Israel and Connie Kleinberg
Sunya and Sanford Kleiner
Leonard and Yorkette Kleinman
Mark and Alexandra Kleinman
Susan Kleinman
Dr. Max Kleinmann
Mr. and Mrs. Seymour Kligler
Sandra and Leonard Klirsfeld
Dr. Otto and Lotte Knoller
Beth and Dr. Joseph Kochen
Martin Koenig
Theodore S. Kohan
Dr. and Mrs. Bertram L. Kohn
Florence and Sheldon Kohn
Arlene and Stuart Kolbert
Dr. and Mrs. Justin Kolnick
Adele and Murray Konecky
Kit and Lori Konolige
Doris and Jonathan Konovitch
Edward and Susan Kopelowitz
Mr. Donald H. Koppel
Ethel and Marshall Korn
Marc Korpus
Rabbi Laurence A. Kotok
Marina Kovalyov
Ruth and Ralph Krainin
Dr. Albert S. Kramer, M.D.
Mrs. Frieda E. Kramer
Janet and Earl Kramer
Lenore Kramer
Meyer Kramer
Sylvia and William J. Kramer
Kenneth and Linda Kraner
Rabbi Abraham Krantz
Oscar and Evelyn Kranz
Mr. and Mrs. Jesse L. Krasnow
Rabbi Benjamin Z. Kreitman
Jay L. Kriegel
Mickey Krulwich
Mr. Laurence Kugelmas
Lisa and William Kulak
Irma and Melvin Kulakoff
Renee Kulick Brodie
Mr. Simon Kupitz
Rabbi and Mrs. Paul Kurland
Rabbi Neil Kurshan
Lillian Kurz and Doriane Kurz
Rabbi Irwin Kula,
Ms. Dana Kurzweil
Rabbi Paul Kushner
Robin and Stuart Kwestel
Professor and
Mrs. Shimon Kwestel
Mrs. Sidney Kwestel
Beryl and Mina Kwitkin
Mrs. Sylvia Lachter
Helene and Dan Lacoff
Jan and Iris Lambert
Elaine F. Landau
Richard S. Landau
Dr. Steven R. Landau
Mark and Anne Landman
Joan Bluestone Landorf
Elliott Landowne
Marion and Sheldon Langer
Mrs. Rose Langer
Mr. Harold Langsam
Ted and Linda Lansky
Dr. and Mrs. Alvin M. Lashinsky
Barry M. Lasner
Emanuel and Adele Lassar
Mr. and Mrs. Meyer Last
Liselone and Richard Laster
Linda J. Laub
Alvin N. Laupheimer
Sherman and Florence Lawrence
Mel and Mindy Lax
Philip Lebowitz, M.D.
Jerome D. Lebowitz
Mark and Madeleine Lebwohl
Dr. Oscar and Vida Lebwohl
Ruth and Paul Lederer
Mr. and Mrs. David H. Lee
Douglas and Nancy Lee
Elaine L. Lee
Mr. R. Randy Lee
Mr. and Mrs. Fredric C. Leffler
Audrey Freshman Lefkowitz
Harold and Marilyn Lefkowitz
Dr. and Mrs. Jacob M. Lehman
Mrs. Sarah Lehman
Eileen and Peter Lehrer
Mrs. James J. Leibman
Eleanor and Sol Leibner
Myriam Siboni Leibowitz
Mr. Milton Leifer and
Mr. Lane Leifer
Mr. and Mrs. Lewis C. Leighton
Barbara and Elliot Leinwand
Louis and Gloria Lempke
Mr. and Mrs. David Lenkowsky
Arthur and Annette Leon
Barry and Karen Leon
Mrs. Lillian Lerman
Rabbi Barry Dov and
Barbara M. Lerner
Ian Michael Lerner
Mr. and Mrs. Kenneth Lerner
Mr. Maximilian Lerner
Mindy and Sheldon Lerner
Yaacov and Abigail Lerner
Dr. and Mrs. Robert Lesser
Jeffrey R. Levenson, DDS
Amy and David Levere
Constance and James Levi
Dr. Aaron R. Levin and
Dr. Leonore Z. Gladstone
Dr. Arthur L. Levin
Chani and David Levin
Lester E. and Evelyn Levin
Mr. & Mrs. Richard Levin, Esq.
Emanuel and Miriam Levine
Ethel and Joseph Levine
Herbert and Arlene K. Levine
Irving and Sylvia S. Levine
Joshua and Sarah Levine
Jules E. and Joan M. Levine
The Paul Levine Family
Richard S. Levine
Richard and Beth Levine
Rose and Harry J. Levine
Roxanne and Eric Levine
Sam Levine
Alice and James Scott Levinson
The Liss - Levinson Family
Mr. and Mrs. David M. Levitan
Mr. and Mrs. Martin A. Levitin
Mr. and Mrs. Ted Leviton
Mr. Jack Levitt
Michael and Lena Levitt
Mr. and Mrs. Eric Levor
Andrew H. Levy
Charles Levy
Eli and Doris Levy
Jack and Beverly Levy
Randy and Jules E. Levy
Thomas Levy
David and Babbette Lew
Susan and Barry Lewen
Bernice L. Lewis
Mr. and Mrs. Richard B. Lewis
Theodore B. Liban
Mrs. Hannah Libman
Howard and Delores Lichtenstein
Andrea and Michael Lieberman
Dr. and Mrs. Jeffrey Liebmann
Dr. and Mrs. Stanley Liebowitz
Sandy and Bruce Lilker
Dorothy F. Linde
Howard and Sharon Lindenauer
Shari and Nathan Lindenbaum
Felix and Marcia Linder
Dr. and Mrs. Louis Linn
Diane and Norman Linzer
Janice G. Linzer
Hedy and Ben Lipschitz
Mr. and Mrs. Solomon Lipschitz
Mr. John P. Lipsky
Alan and Sharon Lipworth
Amy and Michael Liss
Mr. and Mrs. Norman Liss
David and Maggie Lissy
Mr. Jeffrey Litt
Nancy Heller and Roger Lob
Eve Gail Lobel
James M. Lober
Drs. Thomas and Patricia Loeb
Richard O. Loengard, Jr.
Lawrence Alan London
Shirley and Harold London
Leona Lorberbaum
In Memory of Samuel Lossef, M.D.
Joyce and Albert Lotters
Theodore S. Lowenthal and
Beverly Lowenthal and Family
Lynn and Jeffrey Lowin
Mrs. Samuel Lowy
Neil R. Lubarsky, Esq.
David and Teri Lubin
Ronda and Michael Lubin
Stephen and Yael Lubofsky
Ricki G. Lubov
Mayer and Helga Luden
David and Beatrice Luft
Yaffa and Rick Lukash
Michael and Judith Luskin
Harry and Ruth Lutzky
Ira C. and Paula M. Lutzky
Bobbi and Michael Luxenberg
Lester Lyons
Stanley and Ann Lyons

Peter and Carol Mack
Dr. Alfred S. Magaliff
Ms. Elinor R. Magid
Lawrence and Milagro Magid
Dr. and Mrs. Morris N. Magin
Mr. and Mrs. Amnon Maidi
Mr. and Mrs. Simon Maier
Esther and David Malach
Randie and Aaron Malinsky
Jane and Arthur Maller
Bernard H. Manashaw
Maurice S. and Carolyn K. Mandel
Stanley S. Mandel
David J. and Rosemary Mandelbaum
Diane and Sid Mandelbaum
Reva and Dr. Joseph Mandelbaum
Mrs. Reva D. Mandelbaum
The Samuel Mandelbaum Foundation
Ronald and Linda Mandle
Esther Judy Manischewitz
Beth M. Mann
Dr. Rebecca T. Mannis
David and Gail Marcus
Mr. David Marcus
Ivy and Jerry Marcus
Dr. Philip Marcus
Phyllis Kantrowitz Marcus
Rabbi Robert Marcus
Mr. and Mrs. Julius M. Marek
Dr. and Mrs. Irving B. Margolis
Rose G. E. Margolis
Mr. and Mrs. Steven Margulies
Dr. Leonard Ingber and Ms. Celeste Marino
Jeffrey Mark
Susan and Morris Mark
David Markbreiter
Judith and Gregg Marks
Mr. Daniel Bond Martin
Ms. Anneliese C. Marx
Sara Schepps Matschke
Jane Z. Matthews
Jane Mattson-Prince
Ruth and Leonard Mauer
Karen and Alex Mauskop
Joseph N. Maxner
Jonathan and Juliana May
Anne and Charles Mayer
Marc and Meera Mayer
Sandra Mayerson, Esq.
Dr. and Mrs. Alan A. Mazurek
Myron and Claire Meadow
Dr. and Mrs. Conrad Mehler
Gordon Mehler
Edward Meilman
Beatrice Melnick
Mrs. Linda Melnick
Jay J. Meltzer
Nina and Zabathy Meltzer
Paula and David Menche
Dr. and Mrs. Lawrence Mendelowitz
Dr. and Mrs. Alan R. Mensch
Geraldine and Norman Merksamer
Steven and Carol Richards Mermey
Sandy and Jonathan Merrill
I. Leonard and Gilda Messer
Meryl and Robert Messineo
Carol and Avram Metzger
Gloria and Melvin Metzger
David N. Meyer
Dr. and Mrs. Donald C. Meyer
Samuel and Miriam Meyer
Dr. and Mrs. Gordon Meyerhoff
Mr. and Mrs. Ben Meyers
Helene Meyers
Herbert M. and Edith Meyers
Rabbi Joel and Sandy Meyers
Jennifer and Dror Michaelson
William Michaelson
Aura and Marvin Milich
Adam H. Miller
Mrs. Belle Miller
Beverly Carter Miller
Claire and Seymour Miller
David and Susan Miller
Howard Miller
Lynne and Dennis Miller
Marc S. Miller
Michael and Margie Miller
Rabbi and Mrs. Amos W. Miller
Dr. Richard L. Miller
Mr. Russell K. Miller
Sylvia Miller
John C. Millman
Judy and Joel Millman
Irving and Phyllis Millstein
Rabbi and Mrs. Ronald Millstein
Rabbi Adam and Sharon Mintz
Dr. and Mrs. David S. Mintz
Jean and Saul Mintz Family Philanthropic Fund
Judith and Arthur Mintz
David and Seena Miodownik
Hilton and Linda Mirels
Alan and Barbara Mirken
Mr. Jordan M. Mishaan
Mr. Barry S. Feigenbaum and Ms. Karen Misler
Mr. and Mrs. S. Leslie Misrock
Dr. and Mrs. Charles Mitgang
Carl and Sheila Mittler
Gilda and Bertram Modick
Mr. and Mrs. Neil Moldovan
Mr. and Mrs. Hyman P. Moldover
Loretta and Michael Molk
Irene and Fred Molod
Michele and Alan Mond
Dr. and Mrs. Gerald Mondschein
David E. Morewitz
Mr. and Mrs. Alan Morganstein
Muriel Gold Morris, M.D.
Dr. and Mrs. Jacob Mosak
David L. Moses
Manfred and Selma Moses
Tibor Moskovits Family
Bernard Moskowitz
Barry G. Moss
Lonnie and Jay Mostel
Ms. Ronda E. Small
Mr. Ira Wolfman
Gilda and Bertram Mudick
Neal P. Myerberg and Aletha B. Myerberg
Anthony M. Myers
Bernard Myerson
Dorothy and Sidney Nadel
Kathy and Warren Nadel
Murray and Renee Nadel
Edie and Jonathan Nadler
Dr. and Mrs. Gerald S. Nagel
Dr. and Mrs. Albert J. Nagell
Dr. and Mrs. Harris M. Nagler
Mr. and Mrs. Leonard Naider
Robin and David Nankin
Blanche Narby
Mr. and Mrs. Albert J. Nash
Dr. and Mrs. Bernard Nash and Family
Jonathan D. Nash
Mildred T. Nash
Benjamin Nassau
Alisa F. Levin and Charles M. Nathan
Arthur and Miriam Nathan
Mr. Joel D. Kazis and Ms. Sara E. Nathan
Dr. and Mrs. Charles Nechemias
Mark and Bracha Needleman
Mrs. Nancy Fuld Neff
Rahmo Nehmad
Clifford Edward Neimeth
Jeffrey Nelson
Leslie S. Nelson
Mrs. Rae Nemovicher
Gene and Lenore Neuburger
Kenneth and Marguerite Neuhaus
Mr. and Mrs. Jeffrey Neuman
Nathan and Tami Neuman
Rabbi J. Gershon and Esther Neumann
Warren and Janet Newcorn
Mr. and Mrs. Lawrence Newman
Shelly, Warren, Michelle and Michael Newman
Victor Ney and Karen Binder Ney
Michael and Ronna Niederman
Leah and Henry Nieuchowicz
The Nordans
Aileen and Murray Novick
Hal and Amy Novikoff
Max and Mildred Novod
Drs. Noel and Ailene Nusbacher
Mrs. Golda R. Och
Adam H. Offenhartz
Mr. and Mrs. Robert Okun
Henry and Sophie Olshin
Barry Oppenheim, Sara Margoshes and Family
Judy and Lanny Oppenheim
Mr. and Mrs. Louis J. Oppenheim
Senator Suzi Oppenheimer
Mr. and Mrs. Harold Orbuch
Mrs. Edith K. Ordan
Moshe and Cali Orenbuch
Melissa Orenstein
Gary and Sheila Orin
Anne Orloff
Ms. Nadine Orloff
Dr. Bernard and Maria Osiek
Mr. and Mrs. Joseph Osofsky
Mr. and Mrs. Abe Osser
Dr. and Mrs. Mortimer Ostow
Lola and Herbert Ostreicher
Gloria and Murray I. Ostrin
Bruce and Harriet Ostrow
Rabbi Dr. Joseph S. Ozarowski and Family
Joseph and Judith Packin
Martin Packouz
Boris Palant, Esq.
Muriel Dobson Palitz
Carl Kenyon Panero
Wendy and Ira Parr
Sally Pass
Mr. and Mrs. Philip Passin
Mrs. Silvia B. Paulson
Morton Pechter
Mr. and Mrs. Edward J. Pecker
Lois Snitkoff and Hadar Pedhazur
Darren and Jayne Peister
Alice Pekelner
Linda and Phil Peller
Carl M. Pellman M.D.
Gary and Leah Perchick
Ed and Debra Perkes
Andrew Perl, Esq.
Bea and Jay Perl
Peter and Marilyn Perla
Rosalie Rosen and Russel S. Perlman
Rabbi and Mrs. James Perman
Mr. Albert Antonino, Mr. Bernard Pestyner, International Tire Wheel Corp.
Nathan Peters
Col. and Mrs. Yehudah L. Petrover
Idette and David Pfeffer
Judy and Philip Phillips
Sharon and Irving Picard
Nancy Pillet
Arthur L. Pinchuck
Galina and Robert Pincow
Mr. Paul H. Pincus
Cole and Stanley Platek
Dr. and Mrs. Robert Podell
Dr. and Mrs. Stuart Podell
Laurie Ferber Podolsky
Letty and Bert Pogrebin
Sharon and Joshua Polan

Rozanne and Joseph Polansky
Nancy and Martin Polevoy
Rabbi and Mrs. Milton H. Polin
Melvin Pomerantz
Ruth W. Popkin
Gail S. Port
Dr. and Mrs. Yale I. Port
Hal and Sylvia Portnoy
Mrs. Sara S. Portnoy,
In Memory of Jack Posternak
Rose Postilnick
Michael and Randi Potack
Claire and Murray Pressman
Mrs. Sharon Prince
Mr. and Mrs. Steven Prince
Michael A. Pruzan
Linda and Curtis Pulitzer
Dr. and Mrs. David Pulver
Arthur and Ruth Quint
Ellen Deutsch Quint
George and Barbara Quint
Cookie and Stan Quittman
Jane and Nathan Rabhan
Michael S. Rabin
Stephen and Susan Rabinowitz
Paula and Josef Raboy
Ionel Raducanu
Rabbi and Mrs. Myron Rakowitz
Rachel and Isidore Rand
Joseph D. Rapaport
Mr. Martin Raphael
Dr. and Mrs. Samuel Rapoport
Harold L. Rapp
Mr. Harold P. Ratett
Rose and Wolfgang Rauner
Zvulun Ravid
Ms. Ronnie Ellen Raymond
David C. Reamer
Michael and Sharon Rebell
Helyn B. Reich
Mrs. Stephen S. Reich
Steven and Tova Reich
Drs. Suzanne and Robert Reiffel
Wanda and Mark Reiman
Mrs. Mildred B. Reimer
Leopold and Lillian Reiner
Susie and Kurt E. Reinsberg
Nathan and Lorie Reischer
Shari and Jeffrey Reisner
Nechemiah and Sara Gail Reiss
Glenn M. Reiter
Robert S. Reitzes
Norman and Barbara Resnicow
Mrs. Bea Reuben
Richard N. Reuben, M.D.
Mr. and Mrs. Boris Reznick
Stuart M. Riback
Arnold and Arlene Richards
Mindy and Lawrence Richenstein
Leonard and Martha Richheimer
Harold L. Richman
Marilyn and Marshal Richter
Norman and Sonia Riegel

Bathsheva Rifkin and
Howard S. Hochster, M.D.
Ted Rifkin
Robert Rifkind, Esq.
Hon. and Mrs. William Rigler
Iris and Ira Rimerman
Marilyn Kneller and Neil T. Rimsky
Seth Siegel and Rachel Ringler
Lester and Sheila Robbins
Reni Roberts
Ann Green Robison
Mr. Gerald Rodis and
Mr. Milton Sosinsky
Mr. and Mrs. Harold D. Roet
Mena Rokhsar
Lisa and Michael Rome
Rabbi J. Leonard Romm
Seymour and Shirley Romney
Theodore Roosevelt, IV
Arthur L. Rose M. D.
Mr. and Mrs. David B. Rosen
Florence and Robert A. Rosen
Mr. and Mrs. Fredric D. Rosen
Hortense Rosen
Marianne and Arthur Rosen
Seymour and Estelle Rosen
Mr. and Mrs. Michael Rosenbaum
Sandra and Dan Rosenbaum
Barbara Rosenberg
Jay S. Rosenberg
Drs. Maris and Andrew Rosenberg
Mollie and Bill Rosenberg
Mr. and Mrs. Richard Rosenberg
Jason Rosenberger
David and Glenda Rosenblum
Dr. and Mrs. Edward K. Rosenblum
Sally and Martin P. Rosenblum
Steven A. Rosenblum
Mr. and Mrs. Abe Rosenbluth
Alan W. Rosenbluth
Howard N. Wallick and
Freda Rosenfeld
Mr. Philip R. Rosenfeld
Samuel L. Rosenfeld
Stanley and Regina Rosenfeld
Sandra & Michael Rosenfelt
Mr. Martin Rosengarten
Joseph and Betty Rosenstock
Debbie and Judah Rosensweig
Esther and Alvin Rosenthal
Stuart and Susan Rosenthal
Mr. and Mrs. Jeffrey S. Rosenzweig
Ellen and Daniel Roshin
Shana and David Roskies
Carol and Bud Rosner
Mr. Coleman A. Rosner
Joel and Renee Rosner
Richard and Daisy Rosner
Gladys Ross
Ina Marcus Ross
Mildred and Matthew Ross
Dr. Paul and Elaine Ross
Dr. and Mrs. Steven Ross

Mr. and Mrs. Mack Rossoff
Betsy Roth
David Roth
Judith and Jay Roth
Mr. and Mrs. Stuart Roth
Robert P. Rothenberg and
Helene Rothenberg
Anita O. Rothfeld
Mr. and Mrs. James L. Rothkopf
Dr. Ivan K. Rothman
Dr. Merton S. Rothman
Gary and Jill Rothstein
Dr. Sidney N. Rothstein
Jan and Joel Rotner
Reba I. Rottenberg
Dr. and Mrs. Merrill and
Laura Rotter
Steven J. and Robin Rotter
Mr. and Mrs. Joshua B. Rovine
Toby S. Rozen
Isidore and Sylvia Rubenstein
Rabbi Jacob and
Deborah Rubenstein
Marilyn and Barry Rubenstein
Family Foundation
Maxie Rubenstein,
"Mr. Israel of Brooklyn"
Dr. and Mrs. A. Lawrence Rubin
Arleen Rubin
Mr. and Mrs. Arthur Rubin
Bruce Rubin
Dennis and Vered Rubin
Diane Rubin
Gilla P. Rubin
Jeffery Rubin
Joel B. Rubin, Esq.
Joseph H. Rubin
Dr. and Mrs. Marvin K. Rubin
Mindy Rubin
Mr. Richard Rubin
Dr. and Mrs. Steven E. Rubin
Mr. and Mrs. Stuart V. Rubinfeld
Elisabeth Rubinfien
Aaron and Arlene Rubinstein
Dr. and Mrs. Benjamin Rubinstein
Ms. Karen J. Rubinstein
Terry and Jerry Ruderman
Mrs. Augusta Krieger Rudnick
Mr. Herbert Rudnick
Alvin and Marilyn Rush
Edward and Jill Russnow
Norman and Susan Ruttner
Bruce and Karen Sabath
Debbie Sable
Elissa Sable
Jack and Sue Safirstein
Joel Sagall
Gail and Mendy Saidlower
Dr. and Mrs. Michael Salamon
Mr. William M. Abrams and
Ms. Julie M. Salamon
Michael L. Salitan, M.D.
Mr. and Mrs. Egon J. Salmon

Mr. Felix Salomon
Shari and Alex Salomon
Karen and Alan Salzbank
Ms. Audrey M. Samers
Robin and David Samot
Rhonda and Steven Samuel
Marvin J. and June S. Sandberg
Lenore and Leonard Sandel
Nina and Julian Sandler
Mr. Paul G. Sandman
Marilyn G. Sarbin
Arlene Sardell
James A. Sarna
Dr. and Mrs. Richard Sarna
Mr. Irving Sauerhoff
Morton J. Savada
Reuven Savitz
Meri Schachter, M.D.
Donald and Joan Schaeffer
Roy and Marlena Schaeffer
Mrs. Sondra Schaeffler
Mark Schanzer
Rochelle L. Chaiken and
Edward L. Scharfman
Ariel and Irene Scharman
Ed Schary and Anne Hack
Gary H. Schatsky
Jacqueline and Warner Schatz
Mrs. Esther Schechter
Dr. and Mrs. Max Scheer
Michael and Carol Scheffler
Jack W. Scheiman
Mr. and Mrs. J. Scheldlinger
Sandra R. Schenkel
Steven C. Schiff
Michael E. Schimler, MD
Greg and Barbara Schindler
Selma and Nathan Schlanger
Roberta and Raymond Schleicher
Lisa and James Schlesinger
Mrs. Frances A. Schloss
Kate and Arnold Schmeidler
Lorraine and Martin Z. Schmidt
Dr. and Mrs. H. Alan Schnall
Bruce and Carine Schneider
Donald and Pat May Schneider
Philip and Jean Schneider
Mr. and Mrs. Lois Schoenfeld
Zelda Schoengold
Vernon and Joyce Scholar
Philip Schotz
Esther and Jesse Schraub
Mr. and Mrs. Dore Schreibman
Mrs. Marcia Schreier
Naomi Schrenzel
Dr. and Mrs. Lee Schulman
Malkah "Mickie" Schulman
Jolie Schwab and David Hodes
Ruth and Fred Schwalbe
Alisa Schwartz
Allen K. and Barbara R. Schwartz
Rabbi Allen Schwartz
Mr. Leslie Schwartz

Evelyn and Morton Schwartz
Mr. Ira S. Schwartz
Laura Schwartz
Dr. and Mrs. Louis Schwartz
Mrs. Patrice Schwartz
Dr. Yvette Kass Schwartz
Enid and Leon Schwarzbaum
The Reverend David Schwarzmer
Israel G. Seeger
Max B. Seelenfreund
Dr. Julian A. Seewald
Alvin and Judi Segal
Charles W. Segal and
Hannah K. Flamenaaum
Linda F. Segal
Martin and Beverly Segal
Mr. and Mrs. Matthew Segall
Ethel Segerman,
In Memory of
my beloved husband Morris
Lila and Bernard Seiler
Mr. Michael D. Seiler
Michele Seligmann
Mrs. Patinka Kopec and
Dr. Jay E. Selsman
Semlitz/Glaser Foundation
Mark and Marlene Senders
Nathan S. Seriff, M.D.
David B. Shaev, Esq.
Howard S. Shafer
Jean Shafiroff
Howard Gershen and Donna Shakin
Dr. and Mrs. Alan R. Shalita
Renee and Jack Shalom,
Audrey and Steven Shalom,
Edward Baronoff
Irwin Abraham and David I.
Shamah & Sons
Alvin and Betty Shames
Ms. Frances Shames
Morris and Marion Shamos
Deborah and Morris Shane
Shapiro, Chaim Meyer Ichil
Arlene J. Shapiro
Judith R. Shapiro
Madelin and Fred Shapiro
Mitchell and Sara Shapiro
Monica and Sandy Shapiro
Paul Shapiro and
Roberta Kupietz Shapiro
Rabbi Charles Sheer
Allyn C. Shepard
Mrs. Louis H. Shereff
Arthur and Nancy Sherman
Dr. John E. Sherman
Lenore and Neil Sherman
Joel A. Sherrow
Mr. and Mrs. Ned Sherwood
Bonnie and Jay Shevins
Mrs. Stuart A. Shorenstein
The Shragowitz Family
Arlene P. Shulman
Beverly and Jason M. Shulman
Harold and Barbara Shulman
Susan and Perry A. Shulman
Fay and Bill Shutzer
Mr. and Mrs. Stephen Siben
Beth S. Siegel
Jeanne B. and Richard Siegel
Mr. and Mrs. Millard Siegel
Drs. Phyllis and Kenneth Siegel
Debra Siket
Diane Silberling
Ellen and Alan Silberman
Gail and Mark Illan Silberman, M.D.
Lee and Lucy Silberman
Rosalie and Leonard Silberman
Carol and Alan Silberstein
Robert and Carol Sills
Robert and Roberta Silman
Beverly and Paul Silpe
Jerry and Rosalie Silva
Mr. and Mrs. George Silver
Mr. and Mrs. Jack Silver
Dr. Joseph W. Silver
Dr. and Mrs. Lawrence Silver
Doris Silvera
Jeffrey and Susan Silverman
Leon and Marilyn Silverman
Mr. and Mrs. Michael Silverman
Nancy and Irving I. Silverman
Robin and Larry Silverman
The Jacob Silvermintz Family
Bruce and Arlene Simon
Dr. and Mrs. Ely Simon
Henry and Ann Rose Simon
Beatrice and Irving Simpson
Ned and Doris Siner
Gladys Singer
Mr. and Mrs. Lawson Singer
Mr. and Mrs. Michael Singer
Cindy and Lawrence Sipkin
Rabbi Melvin and Lenore Sirner
Mark A. Sirota
Ruth Sirota
Dr. and Mrs. Alan B. Siskind
William Sisselman
Sisterhood Park East Synagogue
Sisterhood of
Seaside Jewish Center
Sisterhood JCC of White Plains
Sisterhood Rockwood Park
Jewish Center
Brandon N. Sklar
Herbert Sklar
Dot and Ed Slade
Arline and Herbert Slepoy
Barry R. Sloane
June Fuller Sloane
Gertrude Slodzina
Lucy Abbowdowdola Smith
Michael Elie Smith
Mr. Paul E. Smith
Mr. Robert I. Smith
Seymour Smith
Betsy and Neal Smolar
Nancy and Arnold Smoller
Yakov and Galina Smotritsky
David A. Sneider, Esq.
Mr. and Mrs. Edward Snyder
Michael and Renee Sojcher
David A. Sokol
Marianne and Marvin Sokol
Sola Optical, USA
Audrey and Bruce Soloff
Carol and Eugene Solomon
Mrs. Florence Solomon
Rabbi and Mrs. Sidney Solomon
Dr. Renee Solow
Jay and Shirley Sommer
Susan and Elliot Sommer
Mr. and Mrs. Herbert Sondheim
Mr. and Mrs. Eric S. Sondheimer
Mr. and Mrs. Sonneborn-Turetsky
Ira Lee Sorkin
Joan Ross Sorkin
Nat and Rosalie Sorkin
Al Spatz
Sherry and Gerald Speal
Jay S. Spector
Leonard C. Spector
Dr. and Mrs. Alan Spiegel
Ruth and Siegmund Spiegel
Saul and Michele Spiel
Ninna and Gerhard Spies
Mr. Lawrence Spiewak
Elliot D. and Pigeon Spiro
Jerome and Linda Spitzer
Mr. and Mrs. Marco Srour
Mr. and Mrs. Abraham M. Stanger
Helen Stark
Binnie D. Stein
Cyndi and Arnold Stein
Florence G. Stein
George and Liesel Carol Stein
Lillian and Avi Stein
Mr. and Mrs. Morris Stein
Norman H. Stein and Sheryl Dicker
Mr. and Mrs. Leslie Steinau
Bettie M. Steinberg
Estelle and Eugene Steinberg
Nina Steinberg
Mr. Selwyn and Susan Steinberg
Mr. Terry Steinberg
Mr. and Mrs. David P. Steinmann
Beatrice Sterman
Harry and Thea Stern
Jessica Stern
Dr. and Mrs. Sidney Stern
Joel Sternbach
Ralph and Edith Sternberg
Marc Sternfeld
Joanne Sternlieb
Mr. and Mrs. Justin B. Israel,
Mr. and Mrs. Charles Israel
Mr. and Mrs. Meier Stessel
Colman Steuer
Sharon and Michael Steuer
Ms. Alice B. Stock
Mrs. Evelyn M. Stock
Dr. and Mrs. Henry Stolbach
Herb and Marilyn Stolove
Lewis and Irene Stolzenberg
Amy F. J. Stone
Bonnie Stone
Gila and Steven Stone
Raphael and Mindy Strauss
Mr. Steven S. Strauss
Dr. and Mrs. Michael Streiter
Sharon and Michael Strongin
Mrs. Harold Strudler
Karin Strumwasser
Rabbi Ephraim H. Sturm
Leslie and Arnold Sucher
David M. Sultan
Mr. and Mrs. Kalman Sultanik
Alexander and Susan Sussman
Dr. and Mrs. Albert P. Sutton
Mrs. Fortune Sutton
Norma and Samuel Sverdlik
Marsha and Michael Svirsky
Ruth D. and Alred J. Swan
Maurice and Marcelle Swergold
Barry and Carol Swidler
Mr. Curtis M. Sylvester
David M. Szonyi
Ronald J. Tabak
Dr. Arthur L. Talansky
Denise and Mitchell Tanzman
Albert and Linda Tarasuk
Leonard and Susan Tarr
Adele and Alvin Tarran
Izzy and Gaile Taubenfeld
and Family
David R. Tawil
Carrie and Jerrold Teitcher
and Family
Mr. and Mrs. Marc Teitelbaum
Dr. and Mrs. Marcel Teitelbaum
Dr. and Mrs. Stephen Teitelbaum
Marvin and Suzanne Tenenbaum
Marian and Aaron Tenenbein
Rabbi and Mrs. Saul Teplitz
Mr. Sammy J. Terzi
Rabbi and Mrs. Albert Thaler
Jerome and Sylvia Thomases
Barbara and Richard Tilker
Kenneth and Bernice Tillman
The Foundation To-Life, Inc.
Dr. and Mrs. Paul Todtfeld
Mr. and Mrs. Richard O. Tolchin
Norman Toporovsky
Lewis and Leslie Topper
Torchiner Woliner
Young Men's Assn.
Muriel and Emanuel Trachman
Ben and Barbara Traub
Fran and Arnold Treff
Drs. Ruth and Eric Treiber
Randy and Harriet Tritell
Bernard and Nita Trugman
Mr. and Mrs. Joseph Tuch

Isaac and Rochelle Tuchman
Martin Tuchman
Rabbi Gordon Tucker and
Dr. Amy Cohn
Robert H. Tucker
Mr. Michael J. Tulman
Andrew J. Tunick
Richard D. Tunick
Mr. Leonard A. Tureff
Mr. Theodore Kravitz
Leon Turovsky, M.D. and
Zina Turovsky, M.D.
Mr. and Mrs. Charles S. Ullmann
Amy Unger and Peter Eisenberg
Max and Florence Uydess
Ellen Grabois Victor
Cecile Freireich Vinik
Moses Vogel
Kurt J. and May R. Vollweiler
Fred and Judith Vorchheimer
Louis and Ilene Vynerib
Mr. and Mrs. Herbert Wagner
George Wailand
David and Pamela Waill
Phyllis and Otto Waldmann
Dr. Jacob Walfish
Mr. Stephen B. Walfish
Susan and Robert Wallach
Ron and Marilyn Walter
The Waltzer Family
Bernard Warach
Irwin H. and Elizabeth Warren
Mr. and Mrs. Peter Warren
Alan B. Wasser
Mr. and Mrs. Alexander
Wasserman
Mr. Leonard M. Wasserman
Louis and Debbie Wasserman
Norma and Burton Wasserman
Rabbi Harlan J. Wechsler and
Naomi Friedland - Wechsler
Susan and Ira Weg
Helen and Jacob Weichholz
Dr. Inga F. Weil
Nancy and Alan Weill
Penny and Jeffrey Weill
Dr. and Mrs. Paul Wein
Alma and Zachary Weinberg
Dr. Barry and Leslie Weinberg
Mr. and Mrs. Harold Weinberg
Harry Weinberg
Robert and Karen Weinberg
Steven and Sharon Weinberg
Lawrence Weinberger
Alan and Ellen Weiner
Naomi and Stuart Weinerman
Ilse and Henry Weingartner
Alan H. Weinhouse
Daniel and Wendy Weinreb
Esther and Bernard Weinreb
Mr. and Mrs. David A. Weinstein
Esther and Baruch Weinstein
Dr. and Mrs. Joshua Weinstein
Madeline and Lawrence Weinstein
Sandra and Werner Weinstock
Donna Sinetar and
Stephen Weintraub
Mr. and Mrs. Moses Weintraub
Barry L. Weisberg
Micheline and Richard Weisbroat
Dr. David and Estare Weiser
Mrs. Aileen Weisman
Baila and Stanley Weiss
Dr. Bernard and Natalie Weiss
Drs. Jay and Lyn Weiss
Dr. Michael and Barbara Weiss
Dr. Samuel and Barbara Weiss
Mr. and Mrs. Simon Weisskohl
Dr. A. S. Weissman
Mr. H. Ronald Weissman
Steven and Rhonda
Fisch Weissman
Howard and Suzanne Weitzman
Dr. Don Well
In Memory of Lillian Wellen
Welling International Corp.
Mr. Charles D. Wellner
Ted and Zelda Wengrofsky
Edith West
Mr. and Mrs. Robert S. West
Westchester Board of Rabbis
Steve and Betti Wettan
Scott Wetzler
Rhona and Arthur Wexler
Dr. Larry White
Helene Bass - Wichelhaus, PHD.
Heidi and Lloyd Widom
Allen and Harriet Wieder
David and Sheila Wiener
Mr. and Mrs. Mark Wiener
Solomon Wiener
Morey and Joy Wildes
Mr. and Mrs. Stanley Wilkins
Janet Y. Willen
Charlotte T. Williams
Judy and Philip Wilner
Dr. and Mrs. Arnold Wilson
Mr. and Mrs. Herbert L. Wilson
Christine Hikawa and
David Windreich
Norman Winer
Robert Winograd
Sheila and Carl Wisotsky
Dr. Harold A. and
Dorothy B. Wittcoff
Jill and Moshe Wolberger
Charles and Julia Wolf
Shimon Wolf
Bruce and Ellen Wolfson
Esther Wolfson
Dr. and Mrs. H. William Wolfson
Philip and Regina Wolitzer
Mr. and Mrs. Elliott Wolpo
Abraham and Ana Wons
Richard M. Wortman
Rabbi David and Beverly Woznica
Rabbi Walter S. Wurzburger
Mr. and Mrs. Haskell Yadlovker
Bev and Bob Yaffe
Neal and Barbara Yaros
Mr. and Mrs. Michael Yastrab
Mr. and Mrs. Steven Yavers
Les and Dorothy Yeamans
Helen and Norman Yellin
Dorothy York
Janet and Jay Yoskowitz
Steven and Debbie Young
Boris and Eugenia Yudanin
Dr. Howard Yudin
Sumner and Hortense Zabriskie
Kirk J. Zachary, M.D.
Mr. and Mrs. Henry Zanger
Mr. and Mrs. Mansour Zarabi
Cookie Zazik
Edith and Edwin H. Zeitlin
Elizabeth and Ernest Zelig
Laurie Zeligson
Bella and Mark Zelkin
Gary and Ruth Zelman
Shelley H. Zelson
Steve T. Zelson
Bernice and Gerald Zibrak
Aaron and Marjorie Ziegelman
Gerald and Judith Ziering
Anna and David Zimmerman
Foundation
Evelyn and Ely Zimmerman
Janet and Mark Zimmerman
Mr. Philip Zimmerman
Richard S. Zimmerman
Norton and Marilyn Zinder
Nathan Zipperman
Bernard and Gitta Zivotofsky
Meir and Ellen Zombek
Myra Miller Zuckerbraun
David and Bibsi Zuckerbrot
Mr. and Mrs. Charles A. Zuckerman
Ariel M. Zwang
Evelyn and Seymour Zwerling
Stanley Zwillenberg
Bernard and Pearl Zyniewski

**THOUGH NOT LISTED IN THIS ROLL OF HONOR, UJA-FEDERATION GRATEFULLY ACKNOWLEDGES THE THOUSANDS OF CONTRIBUTORS WHO DONATED AMOUNTS UNDER $1,000 TO HELP MAKE THE MIRACLE OF *OPERATION EXODUS* HAPPEN.**